The Current State of Sociological Theory

THE
CURRENT
STATE OF
SOCIOLOGICAL
THEORY

A Critical Interpretation

LEON H. WARSHAY
Wayne State University

DAVID McKAY COMPANY, INC.
NEW YORK

INTERNATIONAL STANDARD BOOK NUMBER: 0-679-30283-2
LIBRARY OF CONGRESS CATALOG CARD NUMBER: 75-579
MANUFACTURED IN THE UNITED STATES OF AMERICA
DESIGN BY BOB ANTLER

To Diana, אמא,
Jonathan, and Nathaniel

Foreword

The Current State of Sociological Theory may well appear to the reader as an ambitious title implying an audacious task, for anyone even remotely familiar with the discipline must be struck by the anarchy of ideas, claims, and charges that characterize contemporary sociological theory. It is precisely to this amorphous state of affairs that Professor Warshay directs his efforts and to which he makes an important contribution. Instead of joining the fray on substantive grounds, as most writers on theory are wont to do, the author treats the conflicting and complicated diversity of sociological theory as a unit of investigation. The delineation of identifying themes, trends, issues, and debates as these apply to the entire range of sociological theory—rather than the assessment of the adequacy or correctness of one theoretical position against another—is the feature of this book that distinguishes it from other works surveying the field of sociological theory.

As Professor Warshay notes in the Preface, this book is an empirical study of theory. It provides a comprehensive and integrated overview of the empirical diversity of the field. The author presents, in effect, a guide to theory that functions as a map of the entire area, pointing to the intricate relations of the many diverse parts that make up contemporary sociological theory. Others have developed typologies relevant to sociological theories (often in a rather narrow sense), but the effort here is much broader, encompassing attendant methodologies and research strategies. This broader view enables the author to identify major features of the field: for example, his documentation of the domination of sociology by certain kinds of theories.

Professor Warshay's effort should be understood as a deliberate attempt to investigate theory in its most general expression. This book is not a substitute for a more detailed, comprehensive knowledge of the substantive content of major theoretical positions. Nor does Warshay's strategy imply a short-cut to the mastery of sociological theory, a superficial introduction and exposure to the intellectual traditions of sociology. On the contrary, the book is designed to facilitate a genuine understanding of sociological theory by providing sensitizing resources whereby one can locate specific theoretical knowledge in a broader intellectual whole and thereby better understand the segment of knowledge. The book is certainly not a means of opting out of intellectual commitment: rather, it is an aid for making commitment more intellectually rewarding. Consequently, the book constitutes an invitation and a challenge to delve more inquiringly into the fullness of sociological theory. The greatest value of this book derives from the fact that it provides a basis from which the reader can more intelligibly establish and interpret the nature and character of contemporary theory in its fullest sense, not just the theoretical positions of the relatively self-conscious schools of thought.

A general perspective on the range of sociological theory is especially important in the contemporary setting where particular theoretical viewpoints are often argued or assumed to be equivalent to the whole of theoretical activity. In the discipline's emerging self-consciousness, this book will prove to be a valuable resource.

Ted R. Vaughan

Preface

This volume is about the current state of, and apparent trends in, sociological theory. It is an overview of
theory and of related methodological and political issues,
rather than a detailed study of particular theories.

Theory is here understood in its broadest sense as, for
example, "the symbolic dimension of experience, as opposed to the apprehension of brute fact" (Kaplan, 1964:
294*). Hence, theory will include important concepts and

* References to works cited in the text appear at the end of the
book, beginning on page 179.

typologies in current sociology. It will also deal with
small (specific) theory systems and congeries and large
(general) theory systems and congeries. This work also
emphasizes the area of meta-theory, which is a logical
and philosophical analysis of theory; of theory-method
issues; and of the ethics underlying theoretical activity.

This is an empirical study of theory. That is, I have
sought to report faithfully the current state of theory and
of theory trends. In fact, while examining the materials
and writing and rewriting, some of my original predilections in favor of large theories and momentous issues
weakened. Weakened also were earlier biases against
practical concerns, empiricist (inductive) research, and
exchange and ecological theories. Moreover, earlier appreciation of humanist broader conceptions of experience,
and of humanist innovations and supplements to neo-
positivist and mathematical methodology, was chastened
by the growing realization that positivist narrowness,
prejudice, and intolerance were matched by humanist
self-indulgent subjectivity, terminological debates, and
cult behavior. This book therefore reflects the changed
views about theory that developed during the process of
its writing.

This book is intended for undergraduate and graduate courses in theory. It is also appropriate for senior
and graduate courses devoted to logical, methodological,
and ethical issues in sociology. It may be relevant to
courses in the social sciences and in philosophy that are
concerned with issues in theory, method, and values.
Finally, the lay public will hopefully find interest in the
issues, arguments, and solutions that are treated here.

I wish to express appreciation to the following
former and current students and colleagues who read and

reacted to earlier versions of this manuscript: David Bartelt, Walter Brumm, Derral Cheatwood, Tom Eynon, Andy Fanta, Walda Fishman, Menno Froese, Nason Hall, Joanne Hendricks, Dean Knudsen, Kyriakos Kontopoulos, Florence Mazian, Shirley Palmer, Bob Pankin, Agnes Perry, Fred Preston, Janice Reynolds, Larry Reynolds, Larry Riley, Dick Rising, Leon Shaskolsky, James Otis Smith, Elmer Spreitzer, and Ted Vaughan.

I am thankful to Marge Tavedian and Becky Warfel for their extensive typing.

I would like to commend Irene Glynn of the David McKay Company for conscientious and excellent copyediting.

Edward Artinian, also of David McKay, has shown much sympathy, patience, and morbid humor.

I wish to thank the following journals for permission to include material adapted from my articles: *Sociological Quarterly,* for some material in parts 1 and 2 and chapter 9; *Sociology and Social Research,* for some material in parts 1 and 2; and *Social Science,* for some material in chapter 1.

I am also grateful to Irwin Rinder for first encouraging me to write this.

Finally, I am grateful to Diana Wortman Warshay, my colleague and wife, who carefully edited and criticized the entire manuscript for both style and content. She has always been the better sociologist.

Introduction

Current sociological theory, while showing some signs toward conceptual coalescence, shows even more diversity—theoretical, philosophic, ethical, and political. The theoretical diversity consists not only of a number of large (i.e., general) theories—such as functionalism, conflict, interactionism, and organizational—but also of a far greater number of small (i.e., more specific, topical) theories. Sociologists pay more open attention to the large theories, but particularly in the many subfields of sociology, the small theories guide more actual research.

Sociology, moreover, appears to be far removed from a unifying philosophy. Indeed, the 1960s saw intensification of the older humanist-positivist polarization, one pole (new humanists) challenging the very norms of science, the other pole (neo-positivists) emphasizing science's mathematical and formal side; most sociologists undoubtedly still fall between these poles. Ethical and political diversity is evident in continual debate about the proper role of sociology, organized around criticisms by, and of, radical sociologists.

The trend toward conceptual coalescence is an exception to the general picture of theoretical diversity. Coalescence is evident in verbal and textbook agreement; another example of it is the use of many of the same concepts, as operationally defined, in several different research areas. A related trend is that most research is empiricist (i.e., inductive). While the last means that this research is not explicitly guided by theory, large or small, it also suggests an increasing practicality in research. In doing their research, many sociologists remain detached from controversy over issues in theory, methodology, or values.

Theory finds itself increasingly challenged by problems and issues. Some are more dramatic, such as theory-method and political disputes; others are less so, such as new subfields, renewed interdisciplinary efforts, and comparative sociology. These create further bases for theoretical expansion and heterogeneity which are often followed by new integration attempts that are at best only moderately successful. For those who see theory integration as necessary and to be achieved as soon as possible, the current theoretical scene must be disturbing. To others, the variety in theory is at least interesting and perhaps even a sign of the field's vitality, openness, and greater ability to deal with social complexity and change.

A greater barrier to those desiring theory integration is the likely prospect that the heterogeneity of the subject matter of a given field, say, sociology, requires diversity in theory. Different kinds of social phenomena —for example, small groups, large systems, socialization, crowds, social movements, communities, ecological phenomena, and population movements—require separate theories that fit or match them. Sociology, therefore, may require several different theories (and methods) that must be used alternatively and selectively for different phenomena.

These examples of the diversity in modern sociology may present a confusing picture, particularly to the nontheorist. Perhaps that picture looks particularly blurred from a contemporary perspective; future analysts of today's scene may find more order. On the other hand, sociology has in all likelihood grown to such a degree that it inevitably contains a large number of heterogeneous and often conflicting theories and approaches. This is deplored by some and either tolerated or even appreciated by others (as will be indicated in chapter 5). Perhaps the field has matured sufficiently and can accept this condition.

The following six statements indicate the content and main arguments of this book:

1. Modern sociology is dominated by small theories and empiricism rather than by large theories or schools. Some explanations are offered for this domination and it is treated with some sympathy (chapter 1).

2. Examination of current large theories shows continuing interest in organizational, interactionist, and, perhaps, functionalist theories and increasing interest in ecological, exchange, conflict, and phenomenological theories (chapter 2).

3. Other trends are considered including tendencies

to open systems theories and to integration of consensus and conflict theories. Also examined are renewed directions toward comparative and interdisciplinary sociology. There is the further conclusion that sociology retains a micro orientation despite some macro attempts (chapter 3).

4. The field is polarized philosophically by a (new) humanist-positivist split, this having frustrated the Theory-Method integration hopes of the 1950s. The historic basis for that split is analyzed (chapter 4).

5. Other controversies over theory and method are examined. Sociologists are accused of lagging behind other behavioral and natural sciences in that sociologists almost unanimously retain their expectation, or wish, for a single general theory for all of sociology (chapter 5). The disputes over the appropriate structure or form for theories and over the existence of a single method for all sociology and all science are appraised (chapter 6).

6. The last part of the book attends to perennial ethical and political issues, recently revived in sociology. Chapter 7 evaluates mutual criticisms between radical and liberal (and conservative) sociologists. Chapter 8 discusses some implications of these issues and disputes.

This book, then, presents the current theoretical variety—large theory and small, humanism and positivism (and empiricism), micro and macro analysis, normative and value-free sociology. It also points to areas of coalescence such as conceptual convergence and pragmatic research and theory building. I appreciate the theory, method, and value diversity; I am intrigued by it and am not sanguine about attempts to deny its existence or to apply a single theory (and method) to this diversity. Sociology, more than most disciplines, should expect variety in theory.

Contents

PART **I** *General Theory Trends*

Major texts in sociological theory are organized in a way that apparently gives their readers the impression that the field is divided into several large theories—such as functionalism, conflict, and interactionism (see chapter 2). Most theory courses probably also give this impression. Presumably, the theories are "large" in that they can generalize widely; thus they can be used to study many different kinds of social phenomena (e.g., social movements, groups, culture, competition) and are relevant to many of sociology's subfields (e.g., criminology, urban sociology, medical sociology, and social stratification). Theory texts and courses that give such impression ignore or severely underplay the presence of, and probable domination by, "small" theories, those that do not generalize widely but are limited to narrower topics or subject matter. Further, despite the fact that empiricism tends to be deplored (but is assumed to be giving way before increasing theoretical development and sophistication), most sociological research is undoubtedly empiricist—inductive—and hence uses neither large nor small theories as its explicit basis.

Chapter 1 describes, and tries to explain, the domination of sociology by small theories and, particularly, by empiricism. Chapter 2, after selecting a criterion for large theories, evaluates their current state; its purpose is not to treat the theories in full. In the process, distinctions are made between current, viable large theories and other theories. Finally, chapter 3 is devoted to other characteristics of current theory that have not been explicitly or fully covered in the analyses of small theories, empiricism, and large theories.

1
Domination by Small Theories and by Empiricism

Although theoretical attention is paid publicly to a few large (i.e., general) theories or schools, most actual research does not explicitly use large theory as its basis. Small theories are much more frequently used. More than this, most research is empiricist (inductive) altogether, using neither large theory nor small. This chapter focuses first on the domination of theoretically informed and guided research by small theories and attempts to account for this. This is followed by examination of empiricism in sociology, with some sympathy for its potential for building theory.

SMALL-THEORY DOMINANCE

The current domination by small theories is obscured by the fact that most theoretical attention focuses on a relatively modest number of large theories, schools, or systems. For about two decades, functionalism or "structure-function" theory (or the "general theory of action") has been the foremost, if not the only, theory in sociology. Interactionism, or "symbolic interaction," has long challenged functionalism's claim to theoretical leadership, but it remains backstage. These two large theories are probably the most self-conscious and cohesive; among the remaining large theories, one might also include Marxist, organizational, and exchange. Yet most actual research in the myriad areas of sociology informed and guided by theory makes use of small theories, applicable to circumscribed topics or subfields of sociology.[1]

Here is a partial list of small theories not placed in any particular order but organized in terms of the sociological subfields in which they appear most likely to be used. For example, small theories in crime and delinquency include differential association, differential identification (Glaser), differential opportunity (Cloward and Ohlin), neutralization (Matza), and containment (Reckless). Social psychology includes role theory, reference group theory, empathy theory (Cottrell and Dy-

1. Moreover, among the large theories, structure-function theory has guided very little research, symbolic interactionism somewhat more. It is the less-publicized large theories that have been more actively involved in research—for example, organizational and ecological theories.

mond), dramaturgical theory, and social engagement and alienation theory (Cumming). The field of mass communications features two-step flow theory, S theory, and transact and reactants theories (Dodd). Collective behavior includes emergent norm (Turner) and value-added (Smelser) theories. Marriage and the family, in its studies of courtship and mating behavior, contains complementary needs theory and the principle of least interest. Demography features intervening opportunities, transition theory, and S theory. Urban sociology, in its studies of urban growth, can point to concentric zone, sector, and multiple nuclei theories or models. Social stratification includes status crystallization, and the subfield of small groups features interaction process analysis and social integration theory (Blau).

While the generality of these small or topical theories tends to be narrow, a few have been used in more than one subfield of sociology. Among these might be role, reference group, labeling, least interest, and S theories. Even less confined to one or even a few subfields are game, information, and general (or modern) systems theories.

Practicality as Limiting Theory "Size"

One possible explanation for the prevalence of small theories is the predilection of sociologists, particularly in the United States, to small problems, to applied areas, and/or to subfields of sociology. The narrower and more concrete endeavor is more likely to be defined as manageable and practical. Not many sociologists focus their interests on broad or abstract sociological issues (Glaser and Strauss, 1967:92), at least not for long after they have left graduate school. Evidently, only a small proportion of sociologists is working at grand theory building, overall theory consolidation and integration, and mathematical, logical, and/or rational model building. For every Parsons, Berger, and Blalock, there are many Mertons, Homanses, Baleses, Blaus, Friedmanns, and Dahrendorfs. Most sociologists use explicit theory, when they do use theory, for circumscribed areas or problems. A particular theory may then be discarded when no longer useful, or it may be brought back as needed for a new area or problem.

True, sociologists using smaller theories can argue that, because one often can subsume a small theory under a larger one, they are testing (and thus using) the larger one as well. For example, Smelser's value-added theory presumably fits under functionalism while interactionism claims role, self, empathy, and reference group theories. Moreover, organizational theory is actually a loose family that includes many small theories (see chapter 2, page 34). Yet, unless the small theory is systematically related to the large one, it is only the small theory that is being used and tested.

The large number of subfields within sociology[2] has encouraged the development and use of small theories. Sometimes a subfield will begin with a large theory but eventually make use of, or develop, smaller theories. Of course, it may ignore or eschew theory altogether.

2. Bogardus (1973:148) writes that the number of specialties or subfields has been increasing, a plausible hypothesis but difficult to test. Riley (1960:924) lists 33 "fields of competence" for 1950 and 1959; Simpson (1961:459) has 22 "specialties," both based on compilations from fields listed by Active Members and Fellows of the American Sociological Association in the 1959 *ASA Directory*; Brown and Gilmartin (1969:284), comparing journal output in 1940 and 1941 with that of 1965 and 1966, list 26 "special interest areas," apparently their own classification. Finally, Stehr and Larson (1972:5), using the 1970 *ASA Directory* classification, list 33 "areas of specialization." When one allows for differences in classification (e.g., Are social mobility and mass communication legitimate specialties?) and combination (e.g., Should social mobility be combined, as it has been, with stratification and mass communication combined with collective behavior?), the number of specialties may fall below 20 or rise above 40.

"Middle Range" as Legitimating Small Theories

A second basis for the preponderance of small theories is perhaps the influence of Robert Merton's "middle range" emphasis. Merton, who was to become the most often quoted sociologist in leading introductory texts and professional journals (cf. Bain, 1962:747; Oromaner, 1968:125, 1972:11), had inveighed against both "master conceptual schemes," at one extreme, and "minor working hypotheses," at the other (Merton, 1949:Introduction). To replace these, Merton advanced arguments for "theories of the middle range," defined as "logically interconnected conceptions which are limited and modest in scope, rather than all-embracing and grandiose" (1949:5). In so doing, Merton saw himself following the call made by T. H. Marshall for "sociological stepping stones in the middle distance" during the latter's 1946 inaugural address as rector of the University of London (Merton, 1957b:9). Merton thus set up a continuum, one pole being a "master conceptual scheme" with presumed generalizability to all of sociology and an opposite pole of "minor working hypotheses" with narrow generalizability —and with the preferred "middle range" theories in the middle. Implied also was the idea that the first pole was abstract and macro, the second concrete and micro.

A "middling range of generality" was therefore seen as the only scheme worthy of (1) being named "theory" and (2) being tested. In any case, rather than a premature attempt[3] to emulate an Einstein, or even a Kepler,

---

3. A comment by Fallding speaks to this point, arguing that any deductive theory can be wrong but certainly not "premature." The issue, says Fallding, is not the range of the theory but the kind (1968:36, 39). More recently, Gray argues that while a general theory of behavior (i.e., "master conceptual scheme") might use special theories of behavior (i.e., "middle range" theories) to advantage, it is not necessary that it do so (1972:6).

sociologists should develop a number of special theories
adequate to limited ranges of data. Examples of such special theories are class dynamics, conflicting group pres-
sures, power flow, and interpersonal influence. Gradually
and eventually, these would be consolidated into a more
general conceptual scheme (Merton, 1957b:6–10).

In part of a later theoretical work, Merton modified
his earlier arguments while claiming fidelity to them
(1967:chap. 2 and 1968:chap. 2). First, the ancestors of
"middle range" theory are extended beyond Marshall to
include Mannheim, Mill, Bacon, and Plato. Second, he
sees "middle range" theory (e.g., role-sets) as frequently
consistent with the variety of grand theory extant, namely
Marxist, functional, social behaviorism, integral (Sorokin), and action (Parsons). Finally, he denies that "middle range" theorizing inclines one toward micro theories
which would fractionate the field and make for an anemic
sociological vision (Merton, 1968:56–58, 43, 62–67).

It is particularly on the basis of the last point that
Merton argues against Bierstedt, Dahrendorf, E. K. Fran-
cis, Maurice Stein, and several Soviet sociologists (the
last accusing him of low-order abstraction) and claims
kinship with Durkheim's work on suicide, Weber's on the
Protestant Ethic, Sorokin's empirical tendencies, and the
work of Riesman and Mills. In so doing, Merton is arguing that middle-range theories—such as reference group
—have in fact empirically been shown to generalize very
widely, a change from the original "middling level of
generality" prescription. Second, they now appear to apply to macro as well as to micro structure and, in fact,
several varieties of middle-range theory are being consolidated within a relatively very short time. Merton gives
examples of the presumed consolidation in the areas of
bureaucracy, occupation, delinquency, public opinion,

and demography (1967:61 and 1968:61).[4] Third, in claiming Durkheim, Weber, Sorokin, and others as middle-range exponents in their empirical work, Merton apparently assumes that empirical fruitfulness and application to more circumscribed areas automatically mean that the theories in question are "middle range" ones rather than "master conceptual schemes." In fact, as indicated in the previous paragraph, existing grand theories (which are deemed the real balkanizers of sociology) are, in 1967, seen as "sufficiently loose-knit, internally diversified, and mutually overlapping" so that all are somewhat compatible with, and may encompass, a given middle-range theory (1967:43).

Whether or not one agrees with the above tendencies to imperialism, it is probably fair to say that Merton's argument both named and encouraged a post-World War II trend in theory. That is, Merton's "middle range" emphasis helped stimulate and legitimate small theories. It has also acquired impressive theoretical support (cf. Wallace, 1969:59; Boskoff, 1972:264).

CONCEPTUAL EMPIRICISM

Of more significance to the current state of theory than the domination by small theories is the empiricism of most sociology. Probably the greater part of sociological activity does not explicitly use theory as the basis for research (Warshay, 1971a:25; Willer and Willer, 1973: chap. 1). Theory (large or small) is given lip service at

4. The current plethora of small theories, in fact, implies that Merton's hoped-for consolidation is more limited at this time than he suggests. Actually, he himself approvingly quotes theoretical physicist Richard Feynman to say that even physics is too fractionated to be consolidated (Merton, 1967:48 and 1968:48).

best or is treated with hostility or disdain as unfounded, scientifically dangerous speculation. The role of theory is seen to follow research inductively as its product or summary rather than preceding research as its subject or organizer (cf. Hauser and Duncan, 1959:12–15; Davis, 1959:768; Glaser and Strauss, 1967:chaps. 1 and 2).

In practice, modern empiricism operates on the conceptual level, with most studies seeking to relate empirically at least two, more-or-less operationally defined concepts—e.g., class to political belief, birth order to occupational success, or paternal support and delinquent peers to delinquency. Sometimes, concepts or variables emerge during the data-gathering phase of a study or in the subsequent analysis. Thus, this situation indicates the focusing of much modern sociology around *the concept,* the lowest level of theory. The use of concepts rather than explicit theory as either the focus or outcome of research might well suggest that current sociology is characterized by *conceptual empiricism.* Yet much can be gained from a problem-solving, inductive approach that builds its theory step by step.

The concern for better concepts is certainly not new in sociology. One can cite Small's (1905) list of 48 concepts as basic terminology for the field, Eubank's (1932) decrying of the fact that the total number is at least 332, and Lundberg's (1942) proposal for bringing conceptual order through operational definition. After World War II, Timasheff (1952) attempted to establish a basis for limiting the number of concepts to under 20; Chinoy (1954) developed a concepts-within-concepts organization of the field; and Bogardus (1960) tried to achieve a consensus empirically, naming 52 concepts as commonly accepted in the field. The 1960s saw increasingly analytic treatment of concepts (e.g., Loomis, 1960; McKinney, 1966 and 1970; Nisbet, 1966). In addition, dictionaries of sociology and social science began to appear around the middle of the century (cf. Fairchild, 1944; Mihanovitch, 1957; Gould and Kolb, 1964; Mitchell, 1968; Theodorson and Theodorson, 1969), undoubtedly reflecting more hope than accomplishment. Whether one held a conceptualist and idealist or an operationalist and positivist view of concepts, the explicit concern with concepts as the building blocks of the field was strongly evident and appears to have carried the day. Today, sociologists who agree on little else seem to be in general agreement on at least the names of up to 50 concepts (cf. Bogardus, 1960; Boskoff, 1972:4). Among these might be primary group, role, stratification, community, socialization, norm, cooperation, change, institution, organization, and conflict. This consensus is weak, however; frequent variation occurs in the explicit and implicit definitions of the concepts (e.g., the differential use of "role" by interactionists and functionalists, as indicated in the note on page 33). But this consensus, such as it is, is all we have.

SUMMARY

Sociologists, like people in general, are practical in most of their professional activities. Tendencies to theory and philosophy are unusual, exceptional, or seen as a temporary turn to the "sacred." Sociology's rationale for existence, going back to Comte, Toennies, and Ward, has been intervention for the purpose of solving social problems. This rationale was embodied in the "Durkheim school" at the beginning of this century (Clark, 1972), the London School of Economics tradition of social inquiry, and the relation between research and application characteristic of the "Chicago School" between the world wars (Faris, 1967; Oberschall, 1972). Currently, the rationale has often been cast in the direction of activism, involvement, and relevance. Although the relation between sociology and social problems, issues, and/or policy was variously appraised by different sociological schools and temperaments, few denied that the findings of the field should bear upon society.[5]

Therefore, sociologists have inclined toward problem-orientation and to circumscribed situations or subject matter such as slums, divorce, community health, delinquency, and problems of the aged. Some of this needs to be descriptive and is valuable as such (cf. Bottomore, 1971:32–33). Nevertheless, as Mills (1943) complained decades ago, it tends toward an isolated, fragmented, and elementaristic treatment of social problems and issues. Such treatment is less likely to make use of macro theory, of grand theory, and even of concepts such as structure and culture (though "subculture" might be used to describe delinquents or the aged). Thus, even where explicit theory is used, it is likely to be small or "middle range" (or "lower-middle range").

To summarize this chapter, then, sociology appears to be dominated by small theories and, even more, by conceptual empiricism. First, for the minority of sociologists that explicitly uses theory as the subject of research (i.e., explicitly testing hypotheses derived from a theory), the smaller theory tends to be used more than the more generalizable theory. Second, most sociological research

5. Even Sumner, the epitome of "abstentionism," saw some relevance for social science findings—for example, to show the properly limited spheres for reform and for government protection. Later sympathizers with a Sumner position—such as Giddings, Lundberg, Van den Haag, Catton—favored the application of sociology, but only where sufficient scientific knowledge had been obtained (see chapter 8).

is probably empiricist: it does not use theory at all except as a consequence of research. A related conclusion is that such research remains on the conceptual level, sociologists finding a modicum of agreement in the defining and empirical interrelating of concepts. Finally, this fragmentation of sociological research and analysis may reflect the practicality of most sociologists: they orient themselves toward small, handleable problems.

It probably is just as well that most sociologists remain practical and concrete, regardless of what their more idealistic and formalistic brethren think. Whatever the advantage of large theories, much can be said for the fruitfulness of more limited theoretical, and even empiricist, research.

2 *Eight Large Theories*

This chapter covers *current* large sociological theories. The criterion for inclusion of a theory here is, therefore, popularity in theory texts and other theory sources. Any analysis of the current state of theory obliges one to include currently popular theories rather than only those that are "good." Hence, criteria for the "goodness" of a theory (e.g., testability, empirical fruitfulness, intelligibility, logical consistency, analytic potential, or human relevance) were not used in selecting, but are used in discussing, the theories.

The first section of this chapter discusses the actual selection process of the large theories. The remainder of the chapter turns to the assessment of their current status.

SELECTION OF THE LARGE THEORIES

Theory popularity is defined here as theories or schools receiving significant nomination or emphasis in current attempts at theory classification. Use is made of theory texts organized in terms of classes of theory, of articles that propose such classifications, and of other theory classification sources in which the classification is incidental to the main thrust of the work.

Perhaps the three leading modern theory texts are Martindale (1960), Sorokin (1966), and Timasheff (1967), each of which is largely organized by theory classifications; a more recent text is Turner (1974).[1] Four other attempts to classify theory are found in two journal articles (Duncan and Schnore, 1959; Wagner, 1963), a theory reader organized into "theoretical viewpoints" (Wallace, 1969), and a theory text dealing with "theories

---

1. Martindale's types of theory are positivistic organicism, conflict, formalism, social behaviorism (subtypes are pluralistic behaviorism, symbolic interactionism, social action), and sociological functionalism (subtypes are macro and micro). Sorokin's are nominalistic-singularistic-atomistic (emphases include physicalist and small groups), cultural systems (several subtypes include macro cultural systems and material or technological), social systems (emphases include social action, functional, dialectic, behavioral, and exchange), and by implication, his own "integral" theory (1966:chap. 18). His 1965 article incorrectly lists integral theory as an explicit part of his forthcoming 1966 text (1965:836). Timasheff's are neo-positivism and mathematical sociology, human ecology, functionalism, systematic (emphases include social action and exchange), sociometry and micro-sociology, dynamic, and philosophical (subtypes are phenomenological, institutional, other). Turner's are functional, conflict, interaction, exchange, and, possibly, ethnomethodology.

and theory groups" (Mullins, 1973).[2] In addition to these eight sources, four books dealing with general theory issues (Rex, 1961; Buckley, 1967; Cohen, 1968; Larson, 1973), one with "the development of modern sociology" (Hinkle and Hinkle, 1954), and a theory chapter in a collection on modern sociology (Homans, 1964b) are also used, making a total of fourteen sources for theory classification.[3] The number of theory types in these fourteen sources ranges from three to eleven, with some including classical theories as well as current ones. Moreover, some theory sources break their types into subtypes (Wagner has 54) and, in some cases, the subtypes are used here instead of the types (cf. Martindale, Wagner, Sorokin).

In the fourteen theory sources, the most frequently named schools or theories, in order of descending frequency, are functionalism, macro-functionalism, or structure-functionalism (twelve aggregate mentions in the fourteen sources); social action or Weberian (nine mentions); conflict and symbolic interactionism (seven

2. Duncan and Schnore's types of theory are cultural, behavioral, and ecological. Wagner's are positive (includes ecology and structure-functionalism), interpretative (includes Weberian, symbolic interaction, and phenomenological), and nonscientific or evaluative (includes conflict and neo-Marxian). Wallace's eleven "theoretical" viewpoints are ecologism, demographism, materialism (i.e., physiological), psychologism, technologism, functional structuralism, exchange structuralism, conflict structuralism, symbolic interactionism, social actionism, and functional imperativism. Mullins' "theory and theory groups" are standard American sociology (largely structure-functionalism), symbolic interactionism, small group, social forecasters, ethnomethodology, new causal, structuralists, and radical-critical.
3. Rex's theory types are functional, social action, and conflict (Marxist and other); Buckley's types are mechanical, organic (includes functionalism), and process (includes modern systems theory and symbolic interactionism) models; Cohen's are functional, social action, conflict, and consensus; Larson's are social psychological (includes symbolic interaction and situational), Parsonian (social action and social system), and exchange and field theories. Hinkle and Hinkle's are neo-positivism, social action, and middle range; Homans' theory types are structural, functional, and psychological.

apiece); exchange (six); ecological and micro-sociology (or small groups) (four apiece); behavioral or psychological (three); ethnomethodology, phenomenological, structural, and technological (two apiece); finally, cultural, modern systems, pluralistic behaviorism, materialism (i.e., physiological), and physicalist (one each). Excluded from the tally were terms that did not refer to substantive theory—for example, neo-positivist, macro, organic, dynamic, and middle range. (See table 1 for the theory sources and their theory nominees.)

Following the popularity (i.e., theory source) criterion, functionalism and social action theory, the only ones chosen by a majority of the fourteen theory sources, are evident selections for this chapter. Two further selections, conflict and symbolic interactionism, were selected by half the theory sources. Further, if popularity includes those chosen by a significant minority of sources, then exchange theory (six selections) would be added. Finally, three weaker candidates would be ecological and micro-sociology (four selections apiece) and behavioral (three selections), making for an overall total of eight possible theories or schools.

Nevertheless, there is reason to exclude social action theory (despite its nine selections) and behavioral theory and to modify micro-sociology. References to social action theory tend to be to Max Weber and others whose work relevant to social action theory ended some time ago (e.g., Znaniecki, MacIver, Sorokin, and the earlier work of Parsons). The only references to recent social action theory is to work by Merton, Riesman, and C. W. Mills in Martindale (1960:425–27, 428–34). Hinkle and Hinkle (1954:67–69) mention Merton but with reference to his middle range, theory-method, and functionalist interests. Behavioral (or psychological) theory does not ap-

Table 1. Distribution of Theories Among the Texts

	Function-alism	Social Action	Conflict	Ecological	Symbolic Interaction	Exchange	Other
Hinkle and Hinkle, 1954		a					neo-positivist, middle range
Duncan and Schnore, 1959				a			behavioral, cultural
Martindale, 1960	a	b	a		b		positivistic organicism, formalism, social behaviorism, pluralistic behaviorism, micro-functionalism
Rex, 1961	a	a	a				
Wagner, 1963	b	b	b	b	b		over forty other theories structural, psychological
Homans, 1964b	a						
Sorokin, 1966	c	c				c	nominalistic-singular-istic-atomistic, physicalist, cultural systems, social systems, integral theory, dialectic

							Theory subtype(s) / description
Buckley, 1967	c				c	c	mechanical, organic, process, modern systems
Timasheff, 1967	a	c		a		c	neo-positivism and mathematical sociology, systematic sociometry and micro-sociology, dynamic, philosophical, phenomenological, institutional
Cohen, 1968	a	a	c			c	consensus
Wallace, 1969	a	a	a	a	a	a	demographism, materialism (i.e., physiological), psychologism, technologism
Larson, 1973	a	b			c	b	situational, field
Mullins, 1973	c		a		a	a	ethnomethodology, small group, social forecasters, new causal, structuralists
Turner, 1974	a	a	a		a	a	ethnomethodology
Number of mentions	12	9	7	4	7	6	

Code: *a* = major theory type, *b* = theory as subtype, *c* = emphasis given but not explicitly classified as a type.

pear to be a viable school as it refers to dissimilar phenomena: to social psychology for Duncan and Schnore
(1959), to the psychological propositions underlying
sociology (Homans, 1964b), and to a Homans (Pavlov-
Watson-Skinner) type of sociology (Sorokin, 1966:526–
28). Micro-sociology (or small groups) will be expanded
to become "organizational and small group theories," thus
referring not only to theory and research in intragroup
processes and to formalistic characteristics of groups (e.g.,
Simmel, von Wiese, Moreno, Homans, Bales, T. Mills)
but also to organizational processes as well (e.g., some of
Simmel and Weber, Selznick, Blau, Etzioni). Thus, it
covers much of what the theory sources refer to as micro-
sociology, micro-functionalism, small groups, and the
formal school.

With these modifications, six theories have been
nominated on the basis of popularity for discussion in this
chapter: functionalism, conflict, symbolic interactionism
(to be called just "interactionism"), organizational and
small group theories, exchange, and ecological. Two additional schools or theories are then added: pluralistic behaviorism (Martindale, 1960:chap. 13) and integral theory (Sorokin, 1965 and 1966:chap. 18). Both schools
suffer from undeserved neglect.

The former, pluralistic behaviorism, is a nonself-
conscious but empirically prolific school or theory within
the tradition of Tarde and Giddings and includes some
work that falls under the cultural and technological
schools as well. Much of its ideas and findings have been
incorporated into general sociology. On the other hand,
integral theory enables broader treatment of largely non-
empirical and/or philosophic trends in sociology. Its inclusion allows recognition not only of Sorokin's work but
also can be seen as representative of (1) some of the so-

cial action and macro-sociology inclinations of MacIver, Znaniecki, and Howard P. Becker; and (2) phenomenological and similar philosophic tendencies found in the above men as well as in the work of Gurvitch, Schutz, and Berger and Luckmann.[4]

None of the remaining theories meets the popularity criterion but some are covered to a degree by the other theories: social action theory by functionalism and integral theory; behavioral (or psychological) theory by interactionist, exchange, and organizational theories; phenomenological theory and ethnomethodology by interactionist and integral theories; technological theory by conflict, ecological, and pluralistic behaviorism theories; and cultural theory by functionalism and pluralistic behaviorism.

What follows is not meant as a full treatment of the theories; that would require one or more separate volumes rather than part of one chapter.

THE LARGE THEORIES

Functionalism

Functionalism, a general theoretical position that exists in several disciplines (including biology, medicine, and psychology), goes back in anthropology and sociology at least to Comte and Spencer (cf. Martindale, 1960: 448). Broadly, functionalism means adaptation of social forms to "needs" (personal and social), with culture, social structure, and social integration being thereby created, modified, strained, and otherwise affected. In its more narrow, current sense in sociology, functionalism is

4. One might note that the less empirical the theory, the more likely is it to have received a large number of nominations.

often called "structure-function" theory. As such, it refers to social action and social forms or systems as adaptive to, and fulfilling functions for, personal needs (basic and derived) and social requirements or "requisites." Functionalism's orientation involves (1) the internal relations within a system, i.e., of parts of a system to one another, and of parts to the whole system; and (2) the relation of the total system to its external environment.

Historically, functionalism arose in the rejection of a piecemeal, elementaristic, and descriptive approach to social life for one that emphasized social wholes and adaptation to a variety of needs, problems, and exigencies. Form was to "follow" function. Functionalism has been a broad category including (1) some who explained cultural forms via social and/or personal utility (e.g., Sumner, Malinowski, and Ogburn), (2) others who emphasized social systems in temporary equilibrium (e.g., Spencer, Ward, and Radcliffe-Brown), (3) yet others who featured cultural integration at higher levels (e.g., Durkheim and Benedict), and even (4) a general problem-solving view of society and culture (e.g., Boas and the Lynds).

Yet modern sociology rather narrowly attends more to Parsons and to his former students (in America, primarily Robert Merton, Robin Williams, Wilbert Moore, Kingsley Davis, Charles Loomis, Marion Levy, Neil Smelser, and Alvin Boskoff) who were influenced by his social systems phase. Parsonian functionalism, or structure-function theory, is thus confined to those who adhere to the "action frame of reference" and to the systems and functional problems found in social action, though not all use all four systems (cultural, social, personality, and biological organism) and all four functional problems (adaptation, goal attainment, pattern maintenance, and integration). Merton, for example, has been more micro and social psychological, referring less to large systems; he also has long been concerned with the logic and use of functional theory. Williams, who has emphasized the cultural side, has long worked in race and ethnic relations, institutions, and has turned to the analysis of conflict. Moore has written on economic factors and social change. Davis has studied social change, population, and the logic of functionalism. Loomis has worked in rural sociology, social system typologies, and on a nomenclature for analyzing sociological theories. Levy's work has featured society, social change, theory, and the logic of functionalism. Smelser has stressed change, economic factors, theory, social psychology, and collective behavior. Boskoff has studied rural and urban communities, social change, and theory.

Over the years, structure-function theory has been shifting some of its theoretical commitment, as examination of Parsons' continuing attempts to incorporate all the "behavioral sciences" under one roof attests. Thus, the voluntaristic theory of action (1937) gave way to structure-functionalism (1945), embracing three systems (1951), then advanced to a cybernetic framework (Parsons, Bales, and Shils, 1953:chaps. 3–5; Parsons, 1961a; Ackerman and Parsons, 1966) and four systems (1959a and 1966), occasionally interlaced with biological and evolution models and sporadic reemphasis of the "action framework." The shift was first noted in 1959 (Martindale, 1963), developed by Dubin (1960), defended by Williams (1961:65–66), carefully analyzed by Scott (1963), and more recently referred to by others (e.g., Bruyn, 1966:27; Sorokin, 1966:404, 419, 431–32; Gouldner, 1970:290, 348, 396). All note the loss of voluntarism by 1951 (except Dubin, who cites 1953);

Williams defends the shift from the actor toward "higher order" units by arguing that this was at least balanced by the fact that formulation of the personality system in 1951 filled in the "black box" actor of 1937 (Williams, 1961:65).

Functionalism has had considerable influence in sociology for many years. One measure of this is the use of many of its concepts (e.g., social system, dysfunctional, and affective neutrality) by sociologists in a manner faithful to their meaning in functionalist theory. For example, Parsons' use of "social system" to define sociology is explicitly or implicitly followed by many. Other ways to measure functionalism's influence is in terms of the great amount of reference to its practitioners (e.g., Merton, Parsons, and Davis) in introductory texts (cf. Bain, 1962:747; Oromaner, 1968:125), journal articles (Oromaner, 1969:333, 1972:11), graduate-student reading lists (Keeley, 1964), papers presented at professional meetings, and the content of undergraduate and graduate sociology courses. Finally, functionalism (and/or structure-function theory) has been considered by many to be (1) the leading current theory (cf. Homans, 1964b; Buckley, 1967:1; Wallace, 1969), (2) the only theory (cf. Parsons, 1959b, 1966:chap. 1; Homans, 1964a: 809), and/or synonymous with sociological analysis itself (cf. Davis, 1959)—at least until the late 1960s.

At the same time, functionalism in general, and Parsons in particular, have drawn strong criticism. Earlier criticisms attempted to reform the "excesses" of functionalism; later ones have been more likely to reject the position altogether. For example, earlier critics focused around:

1. Functionalism supposedly assumes that all existing social forms are functional, a complaint lingering

from Malinowski's days and presumably answered by Merton and Levy.

2. It is conservative (denied by Merton and Parsons).

3. It is vague, tautological, teleological, and unscientific (Nagel, Hempel, Brodbeck, Catton).

With time, the second and third criticisms largely remained and more specific (and less friendly) ones were added:

4. The theory is not empirical, operational, or fruitful (Bottomore, Catton, Schrag).

5. It treats change, process, and emergence poorly (Blau, Blumer, Buckley, Wagner).

6. It treats such basic variables as structure and personality poorly (Dahrendorf, Homans, Novikov, Sorokin).

7. It treats power, conflict, and deviance poorly, largely in terms of issues such as nonlegitimacy, pathology, and system strain (Blumer, Buckley, Coser, Dahrendorf, Lasswell, Lockwood, MacIver, Rex, Strauss).

8. It exaggerates the pervasiveness of an overarching set of norms for social action (Buckley, P. Cohen, Douglas, Garfinkel, Homans, Lockwood, Strauss).

Recently, interest in attacking Parsons and structure-functionalism has been decreasing. The attacks tend to focus on the last few of the above criticisms.[5] Functionalism may be declining (cf. Gouldner, 1970:410; Bandyopadhyay, 1971:15–16; Bensman, 1972:viii; Dawe, 1973:46), at least in terms of relative influence, as it faces more competition from other theories. Some rivals to functionalism, such as Marxist theory and social phenomenology,

---

5. For some recent defenses of functionalism, and particularly of Parsons, see Harry M. Johnson (1969:102), Jackson Toby (1971), Victor Lidz (1972:53–63), and Jonathan Turner (1974:ch. 3).

vie with it in theoretical interest and excitement. Others, such as organizational and ecological theories, have been more fruitful empirically.

Conflict Theory

Until recently, conflict theory, particularly Marxist and neo-Marxist[6] sociology, has been a viable sociological theory in Europe, but largely neglected elsewhere. Even outside the Soviet Union and Eastern Europe, Marxist analyses of society have been popular, e.g., in Central and Western Europe. Such analyses have been made not only by sociologists but also by economists, political scientists, historians, and philosophers (cf. Lichtheim, 1965; Gorz, 1967; Kidron, 1970) whose interests and academic training overlap greatly with those of the sociologists. Hence, themes such as exploitation and alienation, as well as class, trade unions, conflict, power, and ideology, dominate their analyses of modern society, international politics, the Third World, and social change.

Elsewhere in the world where sociology has developed (e.g., United States, Latin America, Japan), Marxist sociology had been neglected, treated as unscientific, and/or viewed as alien or dangerous. In the United States, Marxist and neo-Marxist analyses were largely confined to a limited number of isolates and circles—particularly during the cold war—until the return to respectability of

6. Neo-Marxist sociology refers to those who agree with Marxist views on conflict, power, inequality, exploitation, and the need for radical change but who modify one or more of the following: the relative role of economic as against other factors (e.g., political), the dichotomous development of classes, the inevitability of a proletarian revolution, and the likelihood and nature of a final society. These include Bottomore (1956, 1968), Lockwood (1958, 1964), Ossowski (1963), Horton (1966, 1969a, 1969b), M. Zeitlin (1967), Miliband (1969), Habermas (1970, 1971, 1973), Birnbaum (1971), and I. Zeitlin (1968, 1972).

"radical sociology" during the middle and late 1960s. Even then, few Marxist ideas other than those of Marx himself have been studied by sociologists, with the exception of the work of writers such as Bottomore, Habermas, and Marcuse (cf. Sallach, 1973b:135–37).

In contrast, non-Marxist (or "classical") conflict theory has had greater acceptance in the United States and has been a viable tradition in Europe as well. Classical conflict theory posits conflict as a basic social process that is pervasive, inevitable, and has multiple causes and positive (group building, for example) as well as negative consequences. In Europe this tradition goes back to Gumplowicz, Ratzenhofer, and Simmel. In the United States it includes Sumner, Small, and Park.

All sociological conflict theorists, whether Marxist or classical, stress the role of the *political* in group life, group organization and solidarity being seen by these theorists as uniting and using power in the struggle to preserve or extend vital group interests. Moreover, both Marxist and classical theorists criticize culture and idea systems as rationalizations for existing power relations; thus, ideas, values, morality, and rights are secondary and derivative rather than primary and causal. Given their emphasis on process, conflict theorists see change as continual; all social arrangements, therefore, are temporary and fragile. Distrusting public and overt statements, the conflict methodologist focuses on covert social mechanisms.

The difference between Marxist and classical theories inheres in the "progressive," optimistic, revolutionary, and historicist view of the former as against the conservative (at most, liberal) and skeptical outlook of the latter. Marxist and neo-Marxist theorists (such as Bottomore, Colfax, Horton, Lockwood, Marković, Ossowski, the

Zeitlins) see conflict as inherent in social inequality and, viewing human potential as warped by materialistic, capitalist social relations, assume capitalism to be the last stage of (class-based) conflict. In contrast, classical theorists (e.g., Vold, Coser, Dahrendorf, Rex) hold a multidimensional view of conflict (as caused by economic, ethnic, cultural, communal, and other interests) coupled with a more pessimistic view of human and societal possibilities; they see conflict among classes, aggregates, and groups continuing into the indefinite future. Another way of stating this is that Marxists and neo-Marxists share with all exponents of unlimited progress an "abundance" view of human beings, society, and resources; classical conflict theorists have a "scarcity" view, seeing built-in limits and incompatibilities in the human condition that set boundaries to progress and make cycles and fluctuations frequent in social life.[7]

The recent revival of conflict theory, particularly Marxist and neo-Marxist sociology, is one indication of the decline of theories that stress values and norms in sociology. The signs look favorable for its continuing vitality (1) as Marx returns to favor as a "humanist" (cf. Fromm, 1961:1–83; I. Zeitlin, 1968:pt. 3) and some Marxists find something in common with phenomenology (cf. O'Neill, 1972:174; Goodwin, 1973:3–7), (2) as increased Marxist influence is apparent in sociology theory books (cf. Mills, 1962; Lefebvre, 1968; I. Zeitlin, 1968; Gouldner, 1970) and theory courses, and (3) as Marxist and classical conflict sociologists apply their orientations

---

7. Also classifiable as "classical" conflict theorists are Jessie Bernard (1950, 1962), Boulding (1962), Galtung (1964), and Gluckman (1955, 1965), whose emphasis on a multiplicity of processes—competition, conflict, cooperation, negotiation, and others—has a Robert Park flavor about it.

to many areas of social life. (See Vold, 1958, for an early example; see M. Zeitlin, 1967, Goldthorpe and others, 1969, and Kahn, 1970, for more recent examples.)

Yet, intellectual and political barriers prevent conflict theory from becoming the dominant theoretical orientation. Intellectually, most sociologists (similarly to Durkheim or Weber, Cooley or Mead) have seemed content to emphasize interactional, organizational, and norm variables, with conflict seen as a temporary incompatibility, even as an aberration that points to trouble spots needing attention (see chapter 7, page 136, in this volume). Moreover, too strong an emphasis on conflict by sociologists is a threat to the societal and sociological status quo, thus inviting negative sanctions upon conflict theorists until or unless a revolutionary situation should emerge. In sum, only a minority of sociologists is centrally concerned with conflict; the majority focuses on other interests and concerns.

Interactionism

Interactionism is a major rival to functionalism, to "structure-functionalism," and a challenge to the latter's claim to exclusiveness in sociological theory (cf. Rose, 1954:chap. 1, 1962:chap. 1; Blumer, 1962:186). While newer than functionalism,[8] interactionism was a major sociological theory or school long before "structure-function" theory. In the broad sense, interactionism refers to the focus on interaction, language, role, attitudes, and/or self. It thus includes people as diverse as Blumer, Goffman, and Kuhn; Newcomb, Sargent, and Sarbin. In its narrower sense, "symbolic interaction," the approach

8. Interactionism is often traced to Cooley (1902), sometimes to Baldwin (1895) and James (1890).

centers around language as central, as synonymous with interaction, and as the social process within which mind, self, and role-taking emerge.

For symbolic interactionists in particular, the theoretical inspiration was more the "social behaviorism" of Mead (1934) than the work of Cooley or Thomas. The symbolic interactionist position has developed in terms of the following:

1. Social life is an ongoing process of symbolic interaction (Blumer, 1938).

2. Interaction is a problem-solving process whereby social meaning is given behavior (Rose, 1962:5–7) when one stimulates self as he/she stimulates the other. There is a *relational* "sharing" of behavior rather than a mere responding to the other (Meltzer, 1959:31); "joint action" whereby people "construct" their acts so as to fit them to those of others rather than merely acting in common (Blumer, 1966a:540–41) or "releasing" their response (Blumer, 1962:182).

3. Selves, naming, and roles are seen as emerging in interaction, as continually being tested in interaction, and as possible only because human beings can become objects to themselves.

4. Macro concepts such as culture, society, community, and institution (and even small groups) are seen as either nominal categories to be broken down to the interpersonal level or, at best, as limiting frameworks within which interaction occurs (Blumer, 1962:189–90).

5. The appropriate methodology is that of direct study of the interaction process, as in the "participant observation" espoused earlier by Cooley, Thomas, and Park, stressing the point of view of the actors (Blumer, 1962:188–89; 1969).

The past two decades have seen expansion of interactionism's forms, interests, and research activities. Among its varieties might be listed the following:

1. A Blumer school, emphasizing the more subjective aspects of social life (Blumer, the early Strauss, Lindesmith)

2. An Iowa school, stressing self-theory and a positivistic methodology (M. Kuhn, McPartland, Couch, Stewart, Garretson, Mulford, Salisbury)

3. An emphasis on interaction, stressing its coping and problem-solving aspect, with deemphasis on language (Faris, Rose, H. S. Becker, Stone, Stryker, the later Strauss, Lemert, Matza, Deutscher)

4. A role theory view with a cognitive emphasis within a moderate scientific tradition (Newcomb, N. Gross, Biddle, Sargent, A. Bates, Sarbin)

5. A "dramaturgical" school featuring the intricacies of role, self, and image manipulation (Goffman, Klapp, H. Duncan, Messinger)

6. A field-theory version combining Mead, Lewin, and Lundberg (Coutou)

7. An existential and/or phenomenological brand (Pfeutze, Bolton, Natanson, Wagner), stressing the social as "experienced" by the actors and therefore critical of most of social "science" for its neglect of this dimension.

The interactionist outlook appears to lend itself to both naturalistic and subjectivist interpretations. Of the varieties of interactionism discussed above, the Iowa school, the role-theory view, and the field-theory version best fit a naturalistic interpretation; the Blumer school, the dramaturgical school, and the existential-phenomenological one fit a subjective interpretation (cf. Meltzer and Petras, 1970; Reynolds and Meltzer, 1973). Although the period after World War II saw many interactionists seeking a scientific or naturalistic model, the past decade or so has seen some reemphasis on the subjectivist side, particularly from existentialist and phenomenological perspectives. Maurice Natanson, a philosopher with strong sociological interests, has stressed Mead's phenomenological side more than his behavioral emphasis (e.g., 1956:3–4; 1963:282; 1972). Edward Tiryakian (1965:678–86), who calls himself an "existential phenomenologist," interprets his own position as compatible with "mainstream sociology" that runs from Weber, Simmel, and Durkheim to Cooley, Mead and particularly Thomas, then to Sorokin and even Parsons. Norman Denzin (1969) joined the trend toward a phenomenological interactionism by arguing for a synthesis between symbolic interactionism and ethnomethodology. This position has been severely criticized by two ethnomethodologists, Alan Blum and Peter McHugh (1971:98), who argue that Denzin not only misunderstands ethnomethodology but also misses its "analytic character." A last example is Helmut Wagner's (1974) attempt to bring Mead and Weber-Schutz together by reserving the word *sign* for the gestures used in ordinary everyday consensual interaction and, in contrast, the word *symbol* for the more esoteric (poetic, religious) meanings that are more private and/or elusive.

In contrast to attempted syntheses of social phenomenology and interactionism is the recent argument of William Mayrl (1973). He sees interactionism (Mead's, not Cooley's, version) and phenomenology as representing two incompatible perspectives in that Mead began his analysis with objective social interaction whereas phenomenologists begin theirs with the subjective individual. Perhaps Mead's work lends itself to either a naturalistic or subjectivist interpretation because of differing interpretations by others of his terms such as mind, consciousness, and self.

Interactionism, even in its narrowest sense, has variously been seen (1) as a rival to psychological theories —behaviorist, psychoanalytic, cognitive, and field; (2) as a real alternative to functionalism; (3) as the "dynamic" micro companion of the more "static" macro systems theories. Most symbolic interactionists (such as Blumer, Lindesmith, Stone, Strauss) apparently support the first two statements while rejecting the third; they argue that their theory, and the empathic and participant methodologies it requires, stands on its own, tending to be submerged and distorted when treated as a micro version of larger systems. Interactionism, in its narrower "symbolic interactionist" sense, thus remains a divisive force within sociology.

In its broadest sense, interactionism has been integrated into sociology. One example of this is the incorporation of its central concepts into the field.[9] Another example is the extension of interactionist investigations into a variety of settings, as in the work of Strauss, McPartland, Goffman, and Becker in hospitals, schools, mental institutions, prisons, army barracks, monasteries, and other organizational and institutional contexts. Occasional attempts also have been made to repair interactionism's low level of formalization (cf. Rose, 1962:chap. 1; Kinch, 1963; M. Kuhn, 1964; Stryker, 1964; Miyamoto, 1971) an early weakness in the theory that follows from

9. This "incorporation" led William R. Catton (1964:924), who is not an interactionist, to argue that interactionism is therefore not a separate school. On the other hand, Strauss (in Mead, 1964: xii–xiii), who is an interactionist, criticizes the use of interactionist terms (such as self, generalized other, and role) by noninteractionists as too "static" and deterministic.

Mead's roots in pragmatic philosophy (Huber, 1973:278, 281). Nevertheless, interactionism is not quite "establishment sociology" (cf. Bandyopadhyay, 1971:17) in the sense that functionalism and organizational, exchange, and ecological theories are; this may be caused by its "occupationalist" rather than "professionalist" orientation (see Horowitz, 1967a, and chapter 8, page 160, in this volume). Finally, while interactionists are still suspicious of the macro theorizing, elaborate conceptual architecture, and "imperialism" of functionalism, they find themselves more and more accepting of several organizational and small group approaches and, to a limited degree, of social exchange theory as well.

Organizational and Small Group Theories

Of all the large theories discussed here, organizational and small group theories probably is the one most often used in research. The antecedents of the theory are in the work of Weber, Simmel, Mayo, and Barnard. More recently, in the post-World War II decades, its many practitioners come from several disciplines: among others, Bendix, Caplow, Dubin, Etzioni, Friedmann, Selznick, Udy, and W. F. Whyte in sociology; Drucker, March, Presthus, and Simon in related fields.

The theory applies not only to concrete organizations and groups such as factories, welfare agencies, prisons, and political parties but also to any use of "organization" as a model, explicitly or implicitly. These include some studies of small groups, of communities, and of collective behavior such as groups in industry, community power, and the transformation of sect into denomination and church, respectively. The breadth of organizational theory is indicated by the variety of interests it covers. Among these interests are problem solving and decisions;

organizational goals and values; leadership, management, and control; formal organization and bureaucracy; structural and institutional aspects; communication; human relations and the interpersonal level; personality and culture in an organization; organizational growth and development; societal change; and the organization and its environment.

In general, organizational theory represents a middle-range approach, a way-station from which both the micro interpersonal level and the more macro institutional, and even societal, levels can be attempted. A number of varied examples of this approach are given below:

1. There is the Parsons-Bales attempt to relate Parsons' historical and culturally relative institutional analysis to a more analytic scheme of four functional problems based partly on Bales' small group studies and applicable to any social system (Parsons, Bales, and Shils, 1953; Parsons, Bales, and others, 1955).

2. Frederick Bates' position-role distinction (1956) and Merton's similar "role-set" idea (1957a) are examples of a downward move from macro structure.

3. Gouldner's rational-natural dichotomy of bureaucracy (1959a) and his intricate part-whole analysis of social systems (1959b) is another example. In the same vein as the latter analysis by Gouldner, a micro-macro treatment of intergroup cohesiveness has recently been made by Granovetter (1973).

4. There was a shift toward a more macro level in the late 1950s by Theodore Mills, a Simmelian small groups experimenter. Becoming more impressed with the actual complexity of even small behavioral systems, Mills began to consign the small system in *equilibrium* models more and more to the role of merely a limiting, ideal-type case (1959).

5. Parsons clearly shifted to organizational analysis by the mid-1950s (1960:chap. 1, originally published in 1956), eventually related the above four functional problems and their associated collectivities and institutions to the four "levels" of organization of social systems (largely developed by 1957), starting from the bottom "technical" (interpersonal) level and moving upward through managerial, institutional, and societal levels (1959b:7–16).

6. Terence Hopkins tried to integrate Weber's "structural-institutional" view of bureaucracy and Barnard's interpersonal decision making around the idea of systems of authority as problems of compliance (1961).

7. Blau interrelated the micro (Simmel) and macro (Weber, Marx) levels by seeing the macro as emerging out of the micro via indirect exchange. The study develops explanation for macro variables such as organization, status, values, legitimation, and dialectic change (1964).

8. Caplow, building on some of Simmel's ideas (e.g., coalitions, large organizations are more similar to one another than small groups are, an ahistorical and noncultural view of social relations), developed a scheme for handling both structure and conflict that extends and modifies Simmel, and reflects Simmel's approach, method, and style (1954, 1969).

9. The terms "social organization" and "social structure" had remained divisive ones into the 1950s, reflecting the early postwar separation between "pragmatist" midwestern Chicago types, who favored the former term, and "professional" eastern Harvard-Columbia sociologists, who favored the latter term. With the entry of Chicago graduates (such as H. S. Becker, Goffman, Strauss, Wilensky) into studies of organization and of Columbia,

Harvard, and Berkeley graduates (such as Rossi, Blau, Etzioni, Sills) into more micro interests, the pragmatic-professional distinction has been blunted, with coalescence ensuing around interactional and problem-solving versions of structure.

Overall, the micro trend appears to have been the more dominant. Paul Meadows (1967), in an analytic article on organization theory, has written that the bulk of the organizational literature has been more atomistic than global in that it has interpreted organization in terms of some part of the system selected to represent the total system. For example, organization is seen variously as a residual emergent from joint or collective action, as the product of rational and voluntaristic bio-psychological individuals, and as empirically bounded and bonded systems of action. The atomistic model can be seen (1) as teleological organic, using an organism metaphor; (2) as equilibrium, using a mechanical metaphor; and (3) as motivation, which explains wholes in terms of traits or variables of their parts. The last, motivational, takes four forms: technological (Adam Smith rational), consensual (Rousseau sentimental), rhetorical (communication and persuasion), and learning (social learning of motives) (Meadows, 1967:91–95).

Organizational analysis with its associated small group tendencies has been a very popular theoretical trend. First, its emphasis on the "anatomy" or form of social life lends itself to a large domain of social phenomena. Second, the "tangibility" of organizational phenomena coupled with a theoretically parsimonious conceptual commitment appears compatible with a wide range of method and technique, positivistic and humanistic. Among the methodological approaches have been:

1. Field techniques such as case study, interaction observations, and existing documents and records (as in the work of H. S. Becker, Blau, Caplow, Dornbusch, Janowitz)

2. International statistics and historical data (as in the work of Eisenstadt, Lipset, Marsh)

3. The more experimental and/or quantitative and semiquantitative approaches (as in the work of Barton, Coleman, Mechanic, Stinchcombe, Zelditch)

Further signs of viability are the movement of leading sociologists in its direction, the flood of serious analyses (cf. March and Simon, 1958; March, 1965; Rubenstein and Haberstroh, 1966; Meadows, 1967; Mouzelis, 1967; Olsen, 1968; Price, 1968; Zwerman, 1970), and the current status that "organization" has throughout sociology.

Exchange Theory

Exchange theory, which became popular by the mid-1960s (cf. Thibaut and Kelley, 1959; Homans, 1958, 1961; Blau, 1964, 1968), has led to some new research, to much reinterpretation of earlier research, to attempts at logical consistency via formalization of its propositions, and to arguments about the generality of exchange phenomena.[10] The popularity of exchange theory is an addi-

10. Homans sees exchange as applying to many familiar features of elementary social behavior, although excluding behavior such as love and embarrassment (1961:14–15). Blau sees exchange considerations as widely applicable to goal-directed social behavior, therefore excluding some irrational behavior, and possibly being historically and culturally limited as well (1964:5–7). Sorokin disagrees (1966: 543, 550), seeing Homans' theory as limited to "profitable" relationships in a small portion of groups and hardly at all to large organized social systems, thus excluding familistic, altruistic, and coercive relationships; Blau's theory is similarly seen as limited only to a small fraction of interaction (Sorokin, 1966:549).

tional sign of the recent decline of theories emphasizing norms and values.[11]

The roots of exchange theories are in Hobbes, Smith, and Bentham; in some of Spencer, Toennies, Durkheim, Simmel, and Weber; in the economic interpretations of primitive social organization by Malinowski and Mauss; and in the learning theories of Hull and Skinner. In recent sociology, a trend toward exchange-type theories can be found in Homans (1958, 1961), Gouldner (1959b, 1960), Goode (1960), Blau (1964, 1968), Buckley (1967), and in many recent articles. Generally, exchange theory depicts social life as bargaining and negotiation with emphasis on resources, costs, and rewards. In the exchange process, relationships are established that involve mutual trust and an interlocking self-interest. Norms are secondary and are seen as emergents from exchange mechanisms, as depending on a degree of reward, as tending to be utilitarian (e.g., "fair exchange," "distributive justice") rather than abstract (e.g., moral or aesthetic), and as allowing increasingly complex and more indirect exchange. Therefore, norms are but situational elements to be assessed rather than imperative guides to action.

Bartlett Stoodley, in introductory remarks to readings on the "interchange" approach, evaluates the significance of exchange theory. He sees social exchange, or interchange, as introducing

> dynamism into role performance . . . laying emphasis on the situation of action not so much as a stable

---

11. While the Parsonian branch of functionalism, i.e., structure-function theory, gives a central legitimating role to values and the "cultural system," conflict theory, most branches of interactionism, organizational, exchange, and ecological theories tend to ignore values or treat them as derivatives of organization or interaction.

referent for conformity but . . . for bargaining between relevant actors. Social action thus becomes a
matter of negotiation within the field of resources and
deprivations that define the situation. (1962:41–42)

Later in the same decade, Walter Buckley saw ideal exchange models to be (1) interactional, i.e., neither too
normative nor too individualistic; (2) process rather than
structure; (3) ranging from consensus to conflict; and
(4) embracing both persistence and change (1967:
105–6). Some exchange models, however, are more individualistic and behavioristic, stressing learning theories
and efficient causes (e.g., Homans, 1958 and 1961; Thibaut and Kelley, 1959); some are more purely interactional with a strong Simmel or Mead influence (as in the
work of Blau, 1964, 1968; Buckley, 1967) and stress
personal attraction and unspecified obligations; yet others
are functionalist, implying final causes (e.g., Malinowski,
1922:chap. 3, and 1926; Mauss, 1954).

Important similarities exist between exchange theory, on the one hand, and interactionism and organizational theory, on the other. All three theories see norms
as emerging only after stable, reciprocal expectations
have been established. All three emphasize the immediate
situation more than variables from the past. Finally, all
three see themselves as applicable to almost all of social
life, to areas that severely stretch and test the theories. In
the case of exchange theory, this applies in principle to
altruistic and love relationships, at one extreme, and to
coercion (*societas leonina*), at the other. Nevertheless,
behavior under extreme coercion, conformity to inter-
nalized norms, and uncontrollable impulse may be excluded (cf. Blau, 1968:453–54).

Exchange theory has attracted many attempts at formalization as well as critical and logical analysis. Homans has continually advocated this for exchange theory (1958, 1961) as well as for sociology as a whole (cf. 1964b, 1967a, 1967b, 1969). Thibaut and Kelley (1959), psychological social psychologists, were early formalizers of this theory. Blau (1964) has organized exchange theory in terms of a large number of micro and macro propositions under a variety of topics, offering evidence for some propositions and inviting others to test the remainder. Recently, logical examinations of the theory have been made by Bengt Abrahamsson (1970), who is critical of Homans' use of terms and general logic as well; Ronald Maris (1970), who sees Homans' five postulates, together with a few assumptions added by Maris, as adequate for the derivation of twenty-three of Homans' theorems plus seventeen additional theorems derived by Maris; and B. F. Meeker (1971), who uses game theory in translating exchange principles (such as rationality, reciprocity, altruism, group-gain, or status consistency) in order to formalize aspects of exchange behavior.

Recent attempts have also been made to bring exchange theory and symbolic interactionism together. Frank Miyamoto (1971), using the degree of formalization of exchange and balance theories as his goal, tried to systematize interactionist theory by developing a clearer conception of motivation by tying motivation to self-orientation; this concern goes back at least to Nelson Foote's (1951) attempt to bring motivation into interactionism. Peter Singlemann (1972), in contrast, attempted an exchange-interactionism convergence from the standpoint of interactionism, possibly influenced by an earlier criticism that Homans ignores the subjective (Abrahamsson, 1970:283). Exchange processes, while embodying hedonistic goals, were seen by Singlemann to involve actors constructing subjective and socially shared definitions of objects, engaging in role-taking and validation of self (1972). Robert Schafer (1973), disagreeing with Singlemann, says that the Homans version, "reinforcement" exchange, by stressing hedonistic and motivational aspects, can only complement interactionism's subjective and conceptual features of current exchange theories; only Blau's "social" exchange version, by making important modifications in each theory, is seen by Schafer as coming close to a synthesis of the two.

Kunkel and Nagasawa, who are sympathetic to exchange and learning theories, have summarized issues involved in the analysis of exchange (and learning) theories by sociologists and philosophers (1973:532). One issue is the question of phylogenetic continuity (see also Sorokin, 1966:549). A second issue is the logical status of exchange propositions, including the question of their generality (see also Sorokin, 1966:543, 549, 550; Davis, 1973). A third issue is the sparseness, simplicity, and vagueness of exchange propositions. Two other issues have been raised by others; one is the question of logical circularity (Firth, 1965:110; Abrahamsson, 1970:275–77; Davis, 1973:171–72) and the second is that of (Homans') ignoring the subject's private experience (Abrahamsson, 1970:283–84). Yet, exchange theory specifically, and behavioral and reinforcement explanations generally, appear to be gaining in sociology (cf. Burgess and Bushnell, 1969; Kunkel, 1970; Turk and Simpson, 1971; Tarter, 1973; Friedrichs, 1974).

Once the long struggle to establish the reality of social fact had been "won," sociologists became more able to lower their defensiveness (and offensiveness) about sociology's legitimacy and to turn to more modest and less parochial models of social life—such as social exchange.

The hesitant, gradual, but eventual acceptance of socio-logical variables as legitimate and relevant by economists, psychologists, and political scientists—a minority of these even went overboard toward structural and/or normative determinism in the organizational and small group varia-bles they were studying—have made some sociological struggles of less moment. Sociologists could now worry less about dichotomies such as realism-nominalism, emer-gence-reductionism, or structuralism-individualism and feel freer to modify, restrict, and/or abandon normative theories in favor of emphasis upon other processes, in-cluding those found in sister disciplines.

The attention thus began to shift not only to ex-change theories but also to the more behavioral, inter-actional, and organizational analyses such as those of Hughes, Strauss, Turner, and Etzioni—even Parsons' later work (in the 1960s) moved in this direction. Per-haps most closely related to a problem-solving version of small group and organizational theories—and a bridge to disciplines such as economics, anthropology, and psy-chology—exchange theory in sociology is currently very popular and may be at a critical point in its future pros-pects.

Ecological Theory

Originally limited to the study of spatial and tem-poral arrangements of people in relation to their habitat, the early human ecology of Robert E. Park and his stu-dents stressed the ecological or biotic level as separate from the social or cultural level and looked askance upon a more integrated "social" ecology (e.g., Alihan, 1938). Modern ecologists, in contrast, see themselves as general students of social organization, relating social organiza-tions to the natural environment, to population variables, and to technology (cf. Hawley, 1950; Hauser and Duncan, 1959; Duncan and Schnore, 1959; Hauser, 1960; Hawley, 1968). Their focus is a macro problem-solving one on the level of human populations in a specific territory attempting to deal with their environments by using technology to obtain the resources necessary to fulfill their goals (cf. Schnore, 1958:629; Duncan et al., 1960: 3–4; Hawley, 1968; Olsen, 1968:244–47), a perspective influenced by Durkheim. Strong emphasis is placed on locations and functions of human communities and other organized and differentiated groups as parts of larger "ecosystems" (Duncan, 1964; Hawley, 1973) and on populations from a spatiotemporal perspective.

Ecological theory resembles organization and exchange theories in a number of ways. First is the emphasis on economic variables; second is the use of both physical and biological analogy; third is the strong "social engineering" aspect (Hauser, 1969:14); fourth, and perhaps related to the foregoing, the terminology has a similar ring (e.g., "input-output access," "interregional input-output," "interspecies aggregation," and "punctiform agglomerations"). Nevertheless, ecological theory's almost complete deemphasis of variables such as values, norms, and perceptions as less influential upon social organization than are the physical, biological, and technological conditions that brought it into being sets this theory apart from some of the psychological and/or "micro cultural" tendencies of organization and exchange theories. Moreover, ecological theory tends to be more macro than the other two theories. Finally, its tough-minded empiricism—theory being seen as arising out of empirical regularities rather than being speculation, philosophy, taxonomy, or concepts (Hauser and Duncan,

1959:15)—differs somewhat from the greater theoretical fluidity of the above two theories.

Thus, the downplaying of the "behavioral" and "cultural" approaches by ecological theory (cf. Duncan and Schnore, 1959) alienates it from much of current sociological theory, though less from current research. Perhaps the increased social science emphasis upon the physical environment (and the pollution issue) will aid ecological theory's current growth (cf. Hauser, 1969; Catton, 1972; Hawley, 1973).

TWO NEGLECTED THEORIES

Pluralistic Behaviorism

Pluralistic behaviorism is one of the most pervasive, although covert, theoretical tendencies in sociology.[12] Its focus is on social influence more than on social interaction or social structure. It emphasizes repetitive and often similar reactions by many individuals in response to common social stimuli. Also emphasized are such mechanisms as suggestion, imitation, social or cultural conditioning, social habit and custom, and a pluralistic struggle for existence. Examples of this school may be found in many studies of childhood socialization, neighborhood and school influence, occupational folkways, mass influence, waves of fad and fashion, and the diffusion of innovations.

The behavioristic roots of pluralistic behaviorism go

12. The term "pluralistic behaviorism" was applied to this school or theory by Martindale (1960:305), adapting a concept, "pluralistic behavior," seen as the subject of sociology by Franklin Giddings early in this century.

back to Tarde's imitation theory, to the suggestion theories of LeBon and the early Ross, to Giddings' stimulus-response formulation, and perhaps also to late-nineteenth century French psychiatry. The cultural side was emphasized by Boasian anthropology and by several of Giddings' students, most notably Ogburn, Chapin, and Odum.[13] Under the influence of psychological behaviorism and cultural anthropology, a stimulus-response view of social life is presumed, this fitting in well with a cause-effect (or independent variable and dependent variable) model of scientific reasoning. The emphasis on many stimuli and on repetitive individual reactions makes the theory elementaristic which, as Tarde and Giddings argued, lends itself to statistical treatment.

This school represents one of the most popular images that laymen have of the sociological argument, that is, humans are seen as conditioned and overwhelmed by society. Society is depicted as content, an accumulation of custom, belief, emotion, folkways, and the like, often received by mankind passively and uncritically. It is an argument that undoubtedly every sociologist has used at one time or another, if only to impress students and other nonsociologists with the importance of social fact. To argue otherwise would appear to be assuming the primacy of nonsociological variables (e.g., biological, psychological, geography, climate).

Pluralistic behaviorism is less easy to pinpoint than are other schools or theories. Perhaps this is because its many terms (e.g., custom, folkways), mechanisms (e.g., social influence and cultural conditioning), and findings

13. For noted examples of a pluralistic behaviorism approach, one has to go back several decades to Ogburn's and Chapin's studies of social and cultural change, to Odum's regionalism studies, and to Sutherland's "differential association" theory of crime and delinquency.

have been assimilated into general sociology. Rather than a self-conscious school, therefore, pluralistic behaviorism is a label for emphases on one-sided or massive social influence, a passive or socially overwhelmed view of behavior, and study of typical and repeatable (including the typically deviant) behavior.

Integral Theory: Sorokin

Sorokin's integral theory is another neglected theory, a multifaceted one that emphasizes variety in methodology. The name refers (1) to the highest degree of sociocultural integration, for example, civilization; (2) to the highest state of organized sociocultural knowledge; and (3) to a proposed morality. Its scope is broad. It attempts to unite all meaningful social life—in whatever size, shape, and condition—under a single theoretical, methodological, ethical, and activist framework. Its thrust reemphasizes traditions that come from Max Weber and Alfred Weber, from Durkheim (and perhaps Comte), and that have affinity with Spengler, Toynbee, Kroeber, Northrop, and Gurvitch (Sorokin, 1956, 1965, 1966).

Hence, Sorokin focused on (1) meaningful wholes; (2) cultural, social, and personal aspects of these; and (3) integration at the highest levels (i.e., supersystems or civilizations such as sensate or ideational) of "sociocultural reality." Further, the theory includes ideological (meanings-values-norms), behavioral (meaningful interaction), and material (physical and biological vehicles or "conserves") phenomena. Moreover, in distinguishing between social and cultural *congeries* (atomistic or mass phenomena) and organic or sociocultural *systems,* Sorokin also posits a variety of methodologies; statistical and case-study approaches are required for congeries whereas scientific methods and intuition are necessary for systems, with intuition best fitting sociocultural systems at their highest level of integration. Finally, Sorokin offers a total theory of history and a prescription for the future (1966: chaps. 2, 18, and passim).

Given these commitments to idealism, wholism, macro-sociology, and methodological variety, Sorokin's criticisms of mainstream sociology become understandable and predictable. Sociology is criticized for being analytic instead of synthetic, for treating sociocultural wholes in elementaristic and nominalistic ways, for having inappropriate models of social life (e.g., physicalist, mechanist), and, related to the above, for methodological narrowness (cf. Sorokin, 1956, 1958:1127–76, 1965:833–36, 1966:passim). Many of his criticisms of sociology are similar to those made by Znaniecki, Gurvitch, Schutz, Timasheff, and others who hold similar theoretical and methodological outlooks.

Integral theory is foreign to the American experience, flourishing largely in the work of Europeans and expatriate Europeans. Its abstract level of analysis, strong ideational flavor, ideological commitment, and methodological "mysticism" make it an unlikely competitor in the current marketplace. While the deaths of theorists such as Sorokin and Gurvitch have probably weakened this kind of cultural-historical analysis, recent interest in social phenomenology and social existentialism might serve as steps in its revival.

SUMMARY

This chapter evaluated the current state of eight large theories or schools of sociology. It chose six theories according to a popularity criterion, that is, the degree of serious treatment in selected theory sources that classify theories. It presented two additional theories as worthy but neglected theories or schools.

Not all the large theories are highly coherent or self-conscious schools. Nor, as was argued above, are these the main sources of theoretically guided research; only a few are sufficiently research-minded. Their failure to integrate into one theory (see chapter 5) is a further source of disappointment to many, though that would be less crucial if each theory, school, or system was still useful in its own separate sphere. That is, not only have the large theories failed to find a conceptual and logical rapprochement but even their analytic and predictive utility is overshadowed by the superior performance of small theories.

Perhaps the last point, the superior performance of small theories, indicates the most important fact about large theories in modern sociology. For the most part, they are superfluous. They are often pretentious (Dixon, 1973:vii, 116, 120). Large theories fill many articles and books, are seriously studied in professional meetings and college courses, and are evidently very important to their practitioners and to philosophically and theoretically interested outsiders. Except for some of their concepts and ideas, however, large theories appear to be divorced from most sociological activity, the latter consisting largely of empiricist and small theory research leading to lower-level correlations and generalizations (cf. Sorokin, 1965: 833–38, 1966:3–6; Bottomore, 1971:48, 52).

The next chapter supplements the picture presented in chapters 1 and 2. It covers substantive theory trends not treated, or not treated in full, in the preceding two chapters.

3 *Further Characteristics* *of Recent Theory*

A number of characteristics found in current theory cross-cut the small theory–large theory dichotomy. The first of these is a continuing trend toward "open system" or "process" theorizing and away from definition of social phenomena in terms of closed systems (i.e., systems tending to equilibrium and/or homeostasis). In particular disfavor is the positing of social life as closed systems integrated by values and norms. A second and related trend has been an attempt to bring together consensus and conflict theories. This was an effort toward rapprochement between a consensus type of closed system theory—one featuring values and norms; and a conflict type of open system theory—one featuring power, struggle, and rapid change. Third, and related to both the open system–closed system and the consensus-conflict issues, is the movement toward international and comparative sociology, an anthropology-like trend that "tests" Western theorizing. Fourth, and again related to the foregoing, is the increasing interdisciplinary trend in sociology, particularly toward areas relatively neglected by sociologists, such as economics and politics. Finally, despite the macro predilections of both comparative sociology and interdisciplinary trends, sociology remains dominated by micro orientations and elementaristic explanations.

"OPEN SYSTEM" THEORIZING

The past fifteen years have seen increasing criticism of "closed system" and related theories that feature norms and values. Some of this is manifested in continuing criticism of consensus theories by conflict theorists (see pages 60–66), in an occasional psychologistic rejection of social realism (Homans, 1964a), and in warnings of disciplinary narrowness such as Dennis Wrong's "oversocialized conception of man" criticism (1961, 1963). Other critiques have come from serious students of organization such as Gouldner (1959b), Buckley (1967), and Katz (1968), and from students of exchange theory (Homans, 1961; Blau, 1964). Finally, there are those who prefer a "process" approach, claiming kinship with writers such as Simmel, Mead, Park, MacIver, and Sorokin; among these are Hughes, Goffman, R. H. Turner, Goode, Strauss, Garfinkel, and, again, Buckley. Related to the "process" approach are methodological tendencies that might be called humanistic empiricism.[1]

　　In brief, the above critics take closed system theories to task on a number of counts. First, such theories are said to overestimate the unity and interdependence found in social systems—therefore underestimating autonomy, change, and fluidity as well as the prevalence of noncoherent and noncongruent subsystems (cf. Gouldner, 1959b). Second, functionalists in particular treat the dominant structure as legitimate—thus exaggerating the degree of normative integration in systems and treating power, conflict, deviance, and change as residual or breakdown (cf. Buckley, 1967; Strauss and others, 1963). Parsons' definition of power as the "capacity of a social system to mobilize resources to attain collective goals" (1967:225) is a case in point, as is Smelser's definition of collective behavior as "uninstitutionalized mobilization . . . to modify one or more kinds of strain" (1963:71). Finally, closed system theorists do not present a convincing case for the mechanisms that ensure the persistence and/or legitimacy of the dominant structure beyond "natural" tendencies and strains to order, equilibrium, consistency, and rationality. To correct the above theoretical "errors," open system theorists argue that it is better to treat consensus, organization, interdependence, and authority as problematic, as complex and changing relationships that exist in degree and that emerge and disappear with changes in life conditions (e.g., Buckley, 1967: chap. 3; Blumer, 1971:299–300).

　　Three examples of "open system" theorizing are presented here. One is an "autonomous" conceptualization

---

1. Cf. Cicourel, 1964; Bruyn, 1966; Sjoberg and Nett, 1968; Filstead, 1970; Lofland, 1971. See chapter 4 in this volume for discussion of these methodological tendencies.

of organization by Gouldner, apparently one step toward his later theoretical shift to Marxist and/or "reflexive" sociology. Second is Buckley's Modern Systems theory, an open systems approach that, like Gouldner's, remains within the scientific tradition while going beyond physicalist and biological conceptions of, and limits on, science. Third is Garfinkel's emphasis on complex, fluid, and unstated understandings of ordinary daily interaction, an approach that implies "nonscientific" methodologies. The purpose is not to agree or disagree with these writers but to present their work as examples of a partial, and needed, trend away from the extensive preoccupation with equilibrium models.

Autonomy and Reciprocity in Functional Analysis: Gouldner

Over a decade ago, Alvin Gouldner—product of the "Columbia school" but fully cognizant of other (e.g., Midwest) traditions—criticized the facile a priori definition of macro systems and also the assumption that interdependence and equilibrium are intercorrelated aspects of all systems (1959b). As obvious examples of lack of such correlation, Gouldner presents: (1) the *insulation principle,* i.e., low interdependence of subparts of a system may coexist with high equilibrium since, by permitting localized absorption of externally induced trauma, equilibrium of the total system is increased; and (2) *negative feedback,* i.e., high interdependence could coexist with low equilibrium, the "vicious cycle" being an example (1959b:253–54). A related point, that weak micro ties may enhance macro cohesiveness, has more recently been made by Granovetter (1973).

Another Gouldner argument is that reciprocity and autonomy should be treated as variables. For example, stressing not only the consequences of the parts for the whole but also of the whole for the parts, Gouldner found much "assymetric reciprocity" buttressed by compensatory mechanisms such as unconstrained generosity, feudal noblesse oblige, Roman "clemency," power arrangements, and complex generalized-indirect interchange (1959b:249–51). Blau's (1964) later analysis of imbalance in exchange relationships was to be a further development of this idea.

Turning to autonomy as the reciprocal of interdependence, Gouldner analyzed the many kinds and degrees of part-whole autonomy, showing this type of autonomy to be frequently functional and allowing for *dedifferentiation* as an alternative to either system dissolution or radical structural reorganization. Autonomy is prominent not only in "limited purpose" institutions but also in "total" institutions (1959b:254–63). Among functionalists, Gouldner prefers Merton's strategy of *minimal commitment* to an overall system because Merton stresses people in interconnected statuses but avoids macro structure or its "needs" (1959b:242–46).

In all this, Gouldner suggested a dialectic centripetal-centrifugal conflict, naming the work of Hughes, Goffman, and other "Chicago school" products as worthy examples of functional autonomy in organizations. Finally, Gouldner called for factor theories that stress degree rather than kind (of autonomy, reciprocity, equilibrium, etc.), that are translatable into mathematical tools, and that use modern electronic and cybernetic devices that may enable system models to move from vague affirmation of interdependence to an empirical-quantitative weighing of system parts (1959b:254–66).[2]

2. See Fallding's defense of functionalism and his assessment of "process" (1968:chaps. 5, 6).
Gouldner's treatment of social structure in 1959 appears to lie

Modern Systems Approach: Buckley

In 1967 Walter Buckley presented a "soft" version of cybernetics, a "modern systems" approach that is part of Bertalanffy's (1950) general systems theory (see also Bertalanffy, 1968, 1972). Identifying modern systems theory with the "process" model of Simmel, von Wiese, Mead, Park, and Burgess, Buckley goes beyond early versions of information theory to stress a relational view wherein organizations are problematic emergents that exist in degree and that continually rise, fall, and are transformed. In doing this, Buckley sympathizes with Homans' (1961:chap. 18) earlier argument that social norms do not merely survive via habit or custom but must pay their way.

Buckley subsumes modern systems theory under the *process* model, one of three possible systems models (the other two being *mechanical* and *organic*). He rejects (1) the mechanical or equilibrium model which, in tending to equilibrium, typically loses organization (Gouldner's "de-differentiation"); and (2) the organic or homeostatic model, which tends to maintain a relatively high level of organization (1967:8–17). Both models, and particularly the equilibrium, fit only "the very restricted field of 'steady state dynamics' " without growth, evolution, or sudden change (1967:56). In contrast, the process or adaptive model not only sees society as an organization of meanings but posits complex persons with selves —thus putting forth a levels view of both society and person as adaptive, self-regulating systems that include organizational goal seeking (1967:69) defined in

---

between his more standard sociological treatment of topics such as leadership and bureaucracy, in the early 1950s, and his later radicalized and "reflexive sociology" (1970).

terms of efficient causes (1967:79). This model is seen by Buckley as able to handle deviance, conflict, exchange, bargaining, balance, dissonance, strain, and a host of social processes translatable into decision theory (1967:23)—a "fusion of both organicism and mechanism in cybernetics and general systems theory" (1967:37).

Both Gouldner and Buckley are thus strongly critical of Parsons' system. Gouldner criticizes Parsons' obscuring of continua and assumption of only one empirical value for systems. Buckley criticizes Parsons' treating the dominant structure as the norm, as legitimate, as authority.[3] In this, Buckley looks with favor upon Chicago-type ideas such as Ralph Turner's "role-making" and Anselm Strauss and others' "negotiated order." Turner stressed roles as tentative emergents in interaction, varying in definiteness and consistency, and at the mercy of continual interaction in the loose operation of society (Buckley, 1967:146–49). Strauss and his colleagues saw the order found in organizations (e.g., hospitals) as subject to change, as being constantly worked at, reviewed, and altered by parties with dissimilar interests and orientations—a negotiation process within a loose pattern being a better picture of what actually goes on than maintenance of a normatively specified structure (Buckley, 1967:149–51).[4]

3. See, in particular, Buckley's useful distinctions, consonant with MacIver, among power, institutionalized power, and institutionalized authority—the last requiring the followers' "knowledgeable consent" (1967:176–205).
4. A concise statement by Buckley of his position is given in the Preface and General Introduction to his reader (1968). One sign of the spreading influence of general systems theory is its appearance, together with cybernetics and information theory, even in humanist and radical sociology conceptions of the future (cf. Young, 1972). See also Klapp, 1973:286–302.

Ethnomethodology—The Subtle Web
of Social Life: Garfinkel

The idea of an emergent, negotiable, shifting order is further explored in Harold Garfinkel's "ethnomethodology" (1967). Emphasizing the vast web of common-sense understandings and folk classifications that all members of commonplace organized social situations take for granted, Garfinkel still sees these to be in flux. In common with Aaron Cicourel's (1964) and Severyn Bruyn's (1966) preference for qualitative techniques in field research over the more formal, quantitative, and/or experimental approaches, Garfinkel stresses a Diltheylike immersion in social life and a later Wittgenstein (1953) emphasis upon the common understandings underlying simple daily social conversations and transactions. Ethnomethodological investigations study both the biography and purposes of the actors, on the one hand, and analysis of the above common-sense understandings—of the texture of ordinary social life—on the other.

One investigation of this by Garfinkel and his colleagues was to have students record as many as possible of the shared assumptions and understandings behind simple daily situations. A second was a series of experiments in which participants in common situations (e.g., their own family setting) were instructed to act purposely in quite uncharacteristic ways and/or to misunderstand and minutely question the meaning of ordinary statements by naive others, thus eliciting puzzlement, annoyance, and/or hostility from the latter. Sounding somewhat like an anthropologist embarking on a study of an exotic tribe, Garfinkel rejects the use of "rational" approaches that employ formalized methods with precoded entries (1967:38–49; Garfinkel and Sacks, 1970).

More relevant to the above-discussed work of Strauss, Turner, and even Buckley and Gouldner, are Garfinkel's studies to demonstrate that the texture of social life is not a definite and clear norm system of interdependent parts or system-enforcing rules of action by "judgmental dopes" who happily integrate their hierarchy of need-dispositions with a common culture. One of these studies was the questioning of the norm that bargaining for standard-priced merchandise is out of place in modern society. Garfinkel had 135 student-customers go into stores to bargain and found the salespersons often more than willing to lower the price of items, more so in the case of expensive items (fifty dollars or more) (Garfinkel, 1967:68–70).[5]

Ethnomethodology, whose presence was little noticed in sociology until Garfinkel's 1967 text, has since interested many sociologists (among them, Blum, Cicourel, Douglas, McHugh, Sacks, Schegloff, Sudnow, Wieder, Wilson, and Zimmerman) who were dissatisfied with sociological theory and method. Inclined toward the phenomenology of Husserl and Schutz, ethnomethodology has found some compatibility with other phenomenological and humanistic approaches (see chapter 4 in this volume) that emphasize the viewpoint of the actor. Ethnomethodology also fits the recent interest by sociologists (cf. Cicourel, 1964:chap. 8) in the "ordinary language" philosophy of Wittgenstein's later work (1953). That interest is paralleled by a growing interest in sociology among linguistic philosophers whose work derives from the later Wittgenstein (according to Pivčević, 1972:336). Other consonant approaches are the "social construction

5. Three sources of theoretical and methodological issues in ethnomethodology are the readers edited by Jack Douglas (1970), Hans Dreitzel (1970), and David Sudnow (1972).

of reality" (Berger and Luckmann, 1966; Holzner, 1968, 1972) and, to a degree, symbolic interactionism (Natanson, 1963:Introduction; Denzin, 1969). Almost from the beginning, ethnomethodologists have tended toward cultism, both in stressing their differences with outside schools and in arguing among themselves (cf. Coulter, 1971:319; Blum and McHugh, 1971:98).

The writers discussed above are examples of a trend toward treating closed and/or norm systems as problematic. Questions of order, integration, and/or equilibrium are seen as empirical issues, subject to modification and reformulation. Moreover, this trend is not confined to the more loose-jointed methodologies of a Strauss or Garfinkel but is also true of the more "scientific" approach of Buckley or Homans.[6] Nevertheless, when one goes outside sociocultural and social psychological variables to consider biological, demographic, ecological, and physical environment factors, there is more of a tendency toward closed systems (cf. Duncan, 1964; Hauser, 1969; Catton, 1972) and toward scarcity models of social life (see chapter 8 in this volume).

In summation, criticisms of norm and system theories come from a variety of sources: old and new humanists, interactionists, organizational analysts, and exchange theorists. Whether the critics be the above-mentioned writers or others, past and present (such as MacIver, Goode, and Touraine), each in his own way asks such questions as: Are there any systems? What are they? How much order and interdependence (and autonomy)

6. The issue had even become salient to a factor analyst and neo-positivist student of mate selection, Robert F. Winch; in his 1963 revised family text, he showed doubt about the homeostatic model of behavior, until then accepted by Winch and his circle as the only plausible and obvious model to use (1963:v).

exists? functional (or normative) to whom? authoritative and/or legitimate to whom? deviant from what?

CONSENSUS-CONFLICT INTEGRATION ATTEMPTS

Of the more lively intellectual activities in the early and middle 1960s were several attempts to resolve the *consensus* (or functional, normative, equilibrium, order) versus *conflict* (or dialectic, coercion, process) issue. Among the solutions proffered were (1) that both consensus and conflict exist and that both must be studied for a more complete view of society (Dahrendorf, 1959; Horowitz, 1962; Ossowski, 1963; Horton, 1966); (2) that consensus and conflict can be integrated by similarity (Van den Berghe, 1963) or by selection of aspects of each for different kinds of society (Lenski, 1966); (3) that they are intertwined, it being possible for conflict to be functional (Gluckman, 1955; Coser, 1956, 1967; Adams, 1966), to overlap with consensus (Sallach, 1973a), for consensus, in time, to become inevitably dysfunctional (Cole, 1966), and for both consensus and conflict to reach a dialectical synthesis (Friedrichs, 1970, 1974). These three general approaches to the relation between consensus and conflict are examined next.

Both Needed to Complete Societal Picture

Critical of one-sided views, Dahrendorf, Horowitz, Ossowski, and Horton argue for both consensus and conflict models without attempting to integrate them with one another. Ralf Dahrendorf, while bemoaning the neglect by consensus theorists of conflict-producing "substructures" (and seeing conflict theory as necessary to understanding the inevitable conflict of interests within organizations), grants the legitimacy of each to the explication of "Janus-headed" society (1959:159). Irving L. Horowitz similarly criticizes "comfortable" consensual definitions of society and the reluctance of sociologists to study conflict because of alleged methodological difficulties (1962:180). Contending that conflict theory actually applies to more societies whereas the consensus model is really confined to Gemeinschaft, Horowitz calls for emphasis on *cooperation* as a social process that can be variously based upon consensus (internal agreement) or conflict (toleration of differences of interests) (1962: 184, 187–88). Believing both views to be correct is the Polish sociologist Stanislaw Ossowski; for him, each adds knowledge since human societies are complex enough to feature both consensus and conflict (Lenski, 1966:16–20). John Horton criticizes "normative theories" of social problems that define deviance, race riots, and poverty as the inability to realize society's values, seeing this "order" model as part of the "liberal ideology" that dominates modern sociology. Horton calls for a conflict perspective to supplement this (1966).

Integration Possible via Similarity or Selection

Integration by similarity was attempted by Van den Berghe in the early 1960s. After critically analyzing structure-function theory, he proposed the partial reconcilability of dialectic (i.e., conflict) and functionalism (i.e., consensus-order-normative)—and criticized Dahrendorf for accepting both as valid and complementary. Dialectic and functionalist theories are reconcilable in that both are holistic, both contain possibilities for explaining consensus and conflict, and both stress evolutionary change.

Integration by selection was proposed by Gerhard Lenski in an anthropologically-historically based stratification text (1966). Compatible with Van den Berghe's argument that integration of functional (consensus) and dialectic (conflict) theories is an empirical question is Lenski's conclusion that the consensus model fits simpler societies better than the more advanced, whereas the conflict model fits advanced societies better. Lenski's approach to integration contrasts classical *conservative* (functionalist) with *radical* (conflict) views of individual and society and relates these to the historical evidence. Applicable to all societies are *four* conservative assumptions: man as self-seeking, inequality as inevitable, class as usually a nominal category, and work rather than force-fraud-inheritance as determining the distribution of life's necessities. There are also *three* radical assumptions: society as an imperfect system, inequality as usually leading to conflict, and force-fraud-inheritance as largely determining distribution of economic surplus. Conservative (functionalist-consensus) principles dominate hunting and gathering, simple and advanced horticulture, and agrarian societies; radical (conflict) principles better account for distribution in industrial societies, this being the more true where surplus is substantial (Lenski, 1966: passim). Lenski's analysis may explain Van den Berghe's emphasis on long-range tendencies toward integration since the latter was focusing on simpler African societies in his work (Van den Berghe, 1963: note 20).

Intertwining of Consensus and Conflict

More intricate is the analysis of the relations between consensus and conflict by Gluckman, Coser, and Adams. The first two students reason that conflict may often be functional. Gluckman (1955) emphasized institutionalized, ritualized conflict (seeing it as custom-based rather than inherent in all social relations) that aids social integration. Coser (with the backing of Simmel, Cooley, Small, Ross, Sumner, and other early fathers) upheld both positive and negative consequences of conflict (1956, 1967). Like Horton, Coser stresses that the conflict framework emphasizes conflict over central societal goals and values, and the goal of structural change rather than adjustment to the existing values and structure. Complicating the relationship between consensus and conflict was Adams' view that coercion is part of social control, that consensus is one outcome of coercion, and that both coercion and consensus may fit a functional model. He also broadened the emphasis by Gluckman and Coser (even that of others, such as Simmel) by stressing that conflict may be functional to society and dysfunctional to one of its units, or vice versa. Finally, dialectics is a species of coercion theory and conflict is a rebellion against coercion that brings change (Adams, 1966). A more recent and simple argument about possible overlap of conflict and consensus theories is made by David Sallach (1973a). Sallach argues that the two theoretical poles have expanded so that both "critical" (i.e., conflict, dialectic) and the opposing "empirico-analytic" (i.e., consensus, order) theories have both expanded so that each covers change and order. However, each theory still remains different from the other in both epistemology and in contribution to understanding human behavior (1973a:137–38).

A different and novel approach toward intertwining is presented by Robert Cole (1966). He, like Van den Berghe, felt that the issue of integration is an empirical one, but Cole gave empirical resolution a greater role. Rather than comparing theories, Cole argued that the question of whether dialectical or compensating mechanisms are dominant depends upon time and circumstance.

Further, whereas Van den Berghe spoke of a "long-range tendency toward integration" as a convergence of functionalism and dialectic views within an equilibrium model (1963:704), Cole emphasized a dialectic basis for dysfunction. That is, using what is perhaps the most original idea applied to this issue in recent decades, the Sorokin (and Louis Schneider, Wilbert Moore, and many others) "principle of limits," Cole said (1966:45–56) that a given social item may be "functional" at first but eventually "dysfunctional" because "nothing fails like success." What is useful and effective at one time is rigidly retained even when it no longer is effective and even when it becomes detrimental. Hence, a dialectic process of functional, dysfunctional, then a new functional adaptation is frequently the case. No mystical conception of dialecticism is thus needed by this explanation which Cole saw as able to present a fairly convincing empirical argument (1966: 53–57).

However, dialectic consideration is not confined to Van den Berghe, Adams, or Cole. More recently, Robert Friedrichs (1970:51–55, 183–89) has reemphasized a dialectic resolution of the system (consensus) and conflict "paradigms" and points to both European and American tendencies in that direction. Such a resolution is not necessarily cast in Hegelian or Marxist "synthesis of polar opposites" but rather in a more phenomenological awareness of the subject-object relation in science—an interplay between a world produced by "subjective" humans and one that then acts back upon them as an object. In this, Friedrichs' outlook is clearly influenced by Mead, Gurvitch, Schutz, and Berger and Luckmann. However, his more recent feeling is an apprehension that the emerging synthesis of system and conflict theories is likely to be that of Skinnerian behaviorism (Friedrichs, 1974).

If one views Gluckman, Coser, and Adams as reemphasizing an older view of the complexity of "custom and conflict" and the work of Van den Berghe, Cole, and Lenski as fresh attempts to integrate two opposed theoretical positions, there is promise for theory integration. However, Van den Berghe's approach looks only for integration based upon commonality. Lenski's work is less a case of integration than a mechanical synthesis. In his own words, he termed the relation of conservative (consensus) and radical (conflict) a "complex mixture," i.e., a discriminate selection of elements from two traditions (1966:443). The most promising attempt at integration was Cole's more "organic" relation of dialectic to functionalism through time, using ideas of others before him to illuminate this problem. While all three stress the empirical relevance of their integration formulations, Lenski's is the most empirical in that he saw consensus and conflict mechanisms as variables, as varying in degree, as requiring application to both historical and contemporary evidence. Sociologists should then make flexible use of both deductive and inductive evidence as the problem or the situation requires.

A less sweeping approach to empirical theory integration than Lenski's is Jonathan Turner's recent attempt to synthesize different sets of empirical propositions rather than to reconcile basic assumptions (Turner, 1974:chap. 8). Turner rejects working at the level of assumptions for this fails to bring divergent theories together. It involves endless value and metaphysical disputation. Instead, he turns to the empirical propositions of Coser's "functional conflict" theory (extracted from Coser, 1956, 1967, and other sources) and also those of Dahrendorf's "dialectical conflict" theory (taken from Dahrendorf, 1959). By fitting the propositions of these two theorists together and thereby seeing where the propositions support, contradict, and complement one another, Turner hopes that future research will eventually be able to determine the varying conditions for the occurrence of consensus, dissensus, conflict, integration, and the like (Turner, 1974: 121–25, 145–47).

INTERNATIONAL AND COMPARATIVE SOCIOLOGY

Sociology had become largely an American science after World War I. With the death of European scholars such as Durkheim, Simmel, and Weber (and perhaps with the aftereffects of World War I), the center of sociological activity shifted to America, largely to its midwestern universities (Chicago in particular). The period between the world wars in Europe still included a von Wiese, a Mannheim, and a Gurvitch, but America was leading the way, in applied research if not in its theory.

By the 1960s, however, non-American sociology showed definite growth in Europe (including Scandinavia and Eastern Europe), in Asia (particularly India and Japan), and in Latin America. Perhaps aided by economic recovery in Europe and affluence in America, there was an increase in travel, the creation of exchange professors and researchers, and the growth of international conferences.[7] Moreover, there was convergence among countries in that (1) sociological ideas were losing their "national character"; (2) American sociology, whose prewar emphasis was on data-gathering techniques and applied methodology, was developing its theory and conceptualization; and (3) non-American sociology, once

7. For example, attendance at the meetings of the International Sociological Association, held every three or four years, has been progressively increasing, beginning with a few hundred attending in the 1950s to 2,500 in 1966 and 4,000 in 1970 (Janowitz and Hill, 1973:78).

characterized by the study of sociological classics and social thought, was rapidly developing empirical and applied areas.

Coincident with the internationalization of sociology
has been the growth of comparative sociology. This may
be seen in studies of international stratification (cf. Lagos, 1963; Kahl, 1968; Horowitz, 1972); the sociology
of development, of emerging nations, and of "modernization" (cf. Bendix, 1964; Levy, 1966; Ponsioen, 1968;
Nettl and Robertson, 1968; and Horowitz, 1972); and
works specifically in comparative sociology (cf. Andreski,
1964; Eisenstadt, 1965; Moore, 1967; and B. Berger,
1971), including comparative methodology (cf. Przeworski and Teune, 1970). Finally, efforts at cross tabulation
of Murdock's 1957 World Ethnographic sample have
been made by Coult and Habenstein (1965) and of intricate cross-societal analysis and codification by Robert
Marsh (1967). One further example of tendencies to at
least a modicum of international convergence is the increasing study of religion as a legitimate sociological area
among Marxist sociologists in Eastern Europe and Russia
(cf. Birnbaum, 1967).

Greater contact has inclined American sociology toward a more international outlook helped by the many
financial opportunities for overseas travel, research, and
teaching—though these began to dry up by the late 1960s.
In America, there has been more teaching of international
sociology, and conferences, institutes, and book series
around comparative sociology have sprung up. Moreover,
the incidence of cooperative research projects by sociologists of different nations has been accelerating.

Particularly emphasized by these internationalizing
activities has been a slowly developing macro approach.
Given the increasing concern by current sociologists over
political and economic power and conflict, frequently

with a Marxist or neo-Marxist view, there has been some weakening of American tendencies to micro-sociology and social psychology frameworks which are less appropriate to international and comparative research. Another area for macro analysis of a comparative nature may be a renewed interest in social morphology, a form of typological activity that has shown little progress since Durkheim (McKinney, 1970:256).

In the long run, tendencies toward universalism will probably increase with attempts to make theory relevant to many dissimilar societies. That integration of diverse viewpoints will occur is an open question, however, given the difficulty of integrating theories even within a single society.

INTERDISCIPLINARY EFFORTS

A development coincident with trends toward comparative sociology is the increasing interdisciplinary efforts between sociology, on the one hand, and economics, politics, and even biology and the physical environment, on the other. At the same time, social psychology, very popular within sociology for many years, has experienced a relative decline.[8] Part of the "reason" for this may be the shift of micro concerns to organizational and ecological problems—thus making the combination of sociological theory and social organization a more "natural" one than that of sociological theory with social psychology.

8. While social psychology remains the favorite specialty of succeeding generations of sociologists (Stehr and Larson, 1972:5–6), there has been a decline both in the demand for social psychologists (Lavender and Coates, 1972:15) and in publication of social psychology articles in the two leading sociological journals (Brown and Gilmartin, 1969:284).

A second reason may be the apparent lesser relevance of social psychology to problems of international development and to comparative and cross-cultural concerns generally (see pages 66–68). A further possible factor is the revitalization of sociology establishments in Europe and elsewhere with their focus on macro political and economic variables.

Interdisciplinary efforts have a long history in sociology, going back to a focus on (or obsession with) psychology by Durkheim and Gumplowicz or on economics by Marx, Simmel, and Weber. Early American sociologists seemed to be mostly social psychologists (or psychological sociologists)—for example, Ward, Ross, Cooley, Ellwood, Giddings, Thomas—concerned with controversies such as nominalism-realism and reductionism-emergence. Even with the addition of a cultural outlook after World War I by Thomas, Ogburn, Chapin, and Odum, the defensiveness of the field remained—this time manifest in a "putting in their place" of variables such as biology, climate, and geography (cf. Ogburn, 1922; Sorokin, 1928:chaps. 3 through 5). More recently, the trend has been toward a more balanced and less defensive analysis of questions such as reductionism by students in several disciplines.[9]

Hence, the balance of interdisciplinary concerns can be seen to be shifting toward behavioral and social sciences other than psychology and even toward the biological and physical realm. Already mentioned has been the work of the various ecological schools and the "ecosystem" (see pages 43–45), these tying together social organization not only with economic variables but also with

9. In sociology, see Inkeles, 1959; Wrong, 1961; Levy, 1963; and Catton, 1966. In anthropology, see Goldschmidt, 1966:33–49, and Anthony Wallace, 1970:chap. 1 and passim. Also see philosopher Abraham Edel (1959).

geography and spatial variables. Moreover, many developing areas of sociology—e.g., formal organizations, occupations and professions, medical sociology, political sociology, and comparative sociology (cf. Brown and Gilmartin, 1969:284; Stehr and Larson, 1972:5)—have emphasized the relationship with other disciplines, largely in social and behavioral sciences. Many sociologists feel equally comfortable in interdisciplinary pursuits and in obliterating disciplinary boundaries altogether.

Two Parsons' collections in the late 1960s (1967, 1969) are a good illustration of that theorist's continuing and widening attempts to relate sociology to economics, psychology, politics, history, religion, and, to a lesser degree, biology and the physical environment. A further example is the tendency of the sociologist to become a broad social scientist as he or she turns to an increasing number of "applied" areas. It also is a partial answer to Gouldner's earlier criticism (1959b:244–48) that Parsons' "ex cathedra" conceptualization of a social system prior to empirical investigation prematurely excluded the biological human being, the physical environment, and even cultural artifacts—this "charter for an independent social science" proving to be a "Pyrrhic victory" (Gouldner, 1959b:246).

A cautious biological concern was evinced in Robert E. L. Faris's 1961 American Sociological Association presidential address in which he saw the societal supply of "mental ability" as practically limited not so much by genetic factors but by *collective ability* (consisting of technical knowledge, social wisdom, and popular aspirations—all societally determined and group-determined variables) (1961). A stronger bridge to biological variables was made later by Bruce Eckland who, criticizing the overenvironmentalism of sociologists (which he attributed to their liberal political orientation), argued for a real interaction historically between heredity and culture (1967a)—this being consonant with the recent anthropological emphasis that biological evolution has continued into the present together with cultural evolution (see Wallace, 1970:chap. 2; Geertz, 1964:43–47 for examples of this). That Eckland was not merely picking on sociological "straw people" may be seen by Robert G. Anderson's later rejoinder that sociologists should stick to sociological explanations and theories (1967:998), a point noted by Eckland in his rejoinder to the rejoinder (1967b:1000).

In the same year, Jack L. Roach (1967), presenting "a theory of lower class behavior," proposed that sociologists study bio-psychological and nonsocial environmental variables as particularly relevant to the lower class. The more direct exposure of the lower class to unpleasant physical experience and biological privation tends to be downplayed by symbol-oriented middle-class social scientists. Bill Harrell (1967), although not speaking to the lower-class issue as such, presented a stinging criticism of cultural, semantic, and perceptual emphases in the social sciences in an article entitled "Symbols, Perception, and Meaning." In granting the current dominance in sociology and the social sciences of the work of Weber, Thomas, Sapir, Whorf, G. H. Mead, Benedict, and Parsons, he criticized their overemphasis on the role of language, culture, and meaning as mediators between humans and the world of economic, political, and physical reality. Harrell saw these writers offering modern versions of nominalism and idealism. They have replaced "a priori" categories with symbols of historical or cultural content (as did Durkheim) and thus treat social behavior as a symbolic-ideational-cultural filter which is autonomous of the biological, psychological, economic, and physical worlds.

From a different ideological perspective, William Catton has called on sociology to revise its "social construction of reality" paradigm in favor of one giving more attention to biological and ecological factors (1971:81, 83–85; 1972:437). The older, nineteenth-century paradigm saw social and cultural factors as relatively autonomous of biological and physical limitations, as sui generis (1971:84–85, 1972:436–38). Increasing population growth coupled with decreasing resources requires a new paradigm, however, one that stresses not only the uniqueness of the human species because of the possibilities of culture but also human continuity with other organisms because of the increasing limitations of biology, ethology, and the physical environment (1971:83, 1972:438–43). While similar to Roach and Harrell in emphasizing the need to reconsider biological and physical variables, Catton departs from them in that he sees the future to be one of diminished opportunity and luxury, of increased conflict, and perhaps of human extinction (1972:440–46).

The work of sociologists such as Catton and Eckland, together with demographers, ecologists, and students in related disciplines (e.g., Tinbergen, Lorenz, Tiger, Jensen), suggests some renewed interest in *scarcity* models of social life, based upon biological and physical environment variables. Recent "biosociology," "ethology and sociology," "sociobiology," and "sociology and genetics" sections at the American Sociological Association meetings are a further indication of this emphasis.

LATENT MICRO THEORY

Today's sociologist is perhaps less anxious about the status of the discipline both in the academic world and in society as sociology's national and international "relevance" becomes more evident. Thus, the significant recent developments in sociology may include not merely a somewhat more *macro* approach but, more importantly, a greater tendency for nonsociologist and sociologist alike to accept the existence of social structure as a matter of course and to "see" it as "phenomenally real."

Yet one may easily exaggerate the degree of macro study and theorizing in sociology. True, macro theory has been furthered by the rise of comparative sociology (cf. Bogardus, 1973:152, note 3), by some interdisciplinary efforts, and perhaps even by the greater acceptance of the reality of social fact. Nevertheless, micro analysis probably remains dominant throughout sociology, at least as judged by areas of sociological specialization (cf. Stehr and Larson, 1972:5), and even some macro analysis relies on elementaristic explanations of macro phenomena. Some see this as unavoidable (cf. Aage, 1972). But apart from methodological considerations, the micro-macro issue merits attention (cf. Wagner, 1964).

One expects micro theory in studies of self, interpersonal relations, small groups, and the work of some old and new humanists who never wish to lose sight of the individual in social life. Particularly ideological is interactionist treatment of terms such as society, culture, and even group as nominal categories. Too, small group theorists have a long history of assuming their focus to fit larger units without theoretical modification; a good example of the latter is found in the preface to the second edition of Hare, Borgatta, and Bales (1965) where small groups are seen as the key not only to larger social systems but also to culture and personality (1965:v).

Even studies using more macro objects seem to rely on elementaristic explanatory variables, however, as

Meadows has argued (1967:91–95). For example, studies of organizations frequently "sound" like small groups writ large—a good instance being the Berelson and Steiner (1964) inventory of behavioral science findings where in both the "Organizations" and "Face-to-Face Relations, in Small Groups" chapters, many of the same micro concepts and explanations are used. The small group as basic is discussed with approval by W. Richard Scott in his "Theories of Organizations" (1964). Furthermore, Homans' already-mentioned reductionism is clearly a micro approach, beginning with small groups in 1950 and becoming individualistic by the late 1950s (1950, 1958, 1961, 1964a, 1964b, 1967a, 1967b, 1969, 1971a, 1971b), although he did warn against facile generalization from small group to larger organizations in view of the indirectness of exchange in organizations (1961:chap. 18).

One last example of a micro analysis is the reliance on attitude and opinion variables in sociology, long used and criticized. Derek Phillips (1973) is a recent critic while Hans Aage (1972) offers a strong argument in their defense. Phillips partly blames the emphasis on attitudes and opinions by sociologists on faulty methodology —the relying on opinions and perceptions collected by questionnaires and interview schedules—for the current low state of sociology (1973:chaps. 2–4). Aage, in contrast, places the blame for the meager and trivial results yielded by sociological theory on sociology's subject matter rather than on the quality of sociologists or the youth of the field (1972:343). The many variations, exceptions, and random constellations found in social phenomena make those phenomena incapable of incorporation under invariant sociological laws. Hence, attitude variables have been needed, and this appears to be true for the foreseeable future (1972:359–62). Recent emphases by humanist and radical sociologists on phenomenological and personalistic variables promise to continue this trend, whether or not phenomenological variables are integrated into the structural or macro level.[10]

The micro bias is less characteristic of Caplow (1954, 1969) and of the later work of Blau (1964, 1968) and Theodore Mills (1959). It does not hold for many ecological and population studies (e.g., Hawley, Hauser, Duncan, Schnore). It does not hold at all, of course, for many others who focus their analysis upon units extending from large structures through institutions and civilizations (e.g., Sorokin, Gurvitch, Parsons, Etzioni) and on comparative and international sociology (see pages 66–68). Yet the micro level seems more real to most people (Blain, 1971:3–4); it is at any rate part of human primary phenomenal experience. Macro formulations require extra-experience talents, are perhaps beyond human intellectual capacities (Dixon, 1973:30), and raise the issues of not only (1) how to study macro variables such as institutions and cultural values but also (2) the consequence of studying these with methodologies structured for micro variables (e.g., one-way laboratory observations, survey and attitude research, measures of self-concept such as the "Who Am I?").

SUMMARY

The present chapter has dealt with theoretical development that was not covered, or only implied, in the

10. Cf. Young, 1972; Marković, 1972; Goodwin, 1973; Dawe, 1973. See also chap. 4, page 86, and chap. 7, pages 138–39 in this volume.

previous two chapters. Chapters 1 and 2 had a particular concern—small and large theories (and, as it became evident, empiricism). This chapter, on the other hand, dealt with other important trends in theory as well as with issues that cross-cut the small theory–large theory dichotomy. To characterize those trends, there were, first, tendencies to see open system (process) theories as more descriptive of most social life than are closed system theories. Second, several attempts were made to interrelate, even to integrate, consensus and conflict theories. Third and fourth, there were tendencies to apply sociological theory internationally and comparatively, on the one hand, and to move toward other disciplines more than before, on the other. Fifth, and last, continuity with the past was shown in that, despite some macro directions (particularly in international and comparative sociology), most sociological analysis was still micro; even some of the macro tendencies (as in studies of organizations) used elementaristic explanations.

At the end of chapter 2, large theories were deemed mostly superfluous since most sociological activity does not use them but relies instead on small theories and deals in low-level correlations and generalizations. The present chapter has not changed this picture, despite the "higher" level of the issues and interests treated. Traditionally, explanations for this condition have ranged from excusing sociology because of its youth to blaming sociologists. More useful to sociology have been examinations of sociology's subject matter, its methodology, and its moral and political position. Issues such as these comprise the remaining portions of this book.

PART II *Controversies over the Logic of Theory and Method*

Investigation of trends in the logic or philosophy of theory and method provides a perspective of the current state of theory different from the focus on specific theories (chapters 1 and 2) and theoretical trends (chapter 3). Chapter 4 explores a renewed theory-method polarization having strong value implications: the dramatic rise in the 1960s of the "new humanists," at one extreme, and the continually growing "neo-positivist" (formalized, mathematical) sociologists, at the other. The former challenges the scientific tradition and its neutral stance toward "human" issues; the latter seeks to further scientific sociology with physical science as its model and mathematics and formal logic as major tools.

Chapter 5 treats the issue of the existence or desirability of a single (general, integrated) theory in sociology. Surprisingly perhaps, advocacy of a single (rather than multiple) theory finds near unanimity in sociology. Not only do both humanists and positivists generally advocate this, but functionalists and interactionists as well. Yet multiple theory exponents appear to exist in greater numbers in other behavioral and natural sciences, thus suggesting a possible "intellectual lag" in sociology.

The final chapter in this part (chapter 6) examines the question of a single theory structure or form and of a single method for sociology. Both issues divide not only humanists from positivists but also interactionists from functionalists. Thus, positivist plans for a "natural science" of sociology are joined by structure-functionalist advocacy of a "social science," both arguing for a deductive form for theories and a single method for sociology. Opposing this is the position of most humanists and interactionists, who are critical or suspicious of the deductive model for theory and who advocate several methodologies.

Chapters 5 and 6 examine advocates of a single outlook—whether of one general theory, of one theory form, or of a single methodology—and find them wanting. In general, advocates of multiple theories, theory forms, and methodologies present more reasonable arguments. Particular criticisms of single theory advocacy are (1) idealization, that is, offering overly restrictive ideals; and (2) the use of formalistic, rather than pragmatic, criteria.

4 New Humanist and Neo-positivist Sociologies

The issues raised by recent humanist-positivist differences pose questions, in a pure and dramatic way, about the proper course that sociological theory and method should take. They also suggest moral questions, the "new humanists" doing this openly. Further, this polarization bears some relation to the theories and theoretical issues treated in the previous chapters though not every theory would be found at one extreme or the other.[1] Finally, the controversy between new humanists

1. Of the large theories, for example, interactionist, integral, and Marxist theories fall at the humanist pole, ecological theory and

and neo-positivists is but a recent renewal of a sociological debate that goes back to the nineteenth century. A brief tracing of the history of that debate precedes the outlining of the current humanist-positivist debate.

HISTORICAL BACKGROUND

Sociology began as a positivist discipline, if one accepts Comte and Spencer as its effective founders. Comte, and later Spencer, saw sociology as a continuation of the road traveled by the other physical and biological sciences. Gumplowicz, Tarde, and Durkheim in Europe, and Ward and Sumner in America, continued to assume, and often to further, the positivist and natural science model for sociology.

The first major challenge to the scientific model occurred about the turn of the century in Europe in Dilthey's (and, in a more compromising sense, Weber's) opposition to the Ranke empirical, historical tradition. This challenge was not confined to history but extended to empiricist and positivist traditions in the social sciences, including that of Comte and Durkheim in sociology. In classifying psychology and social science as "cultural sciences" which, like history, study unique meaningful configurations with humanistic methodologies, Dilthey took them outside the natural science tradition. In America, an outlook similar to Dilthey's was held by Charles Cooley both before and, particularly, after World War

---

pluralistic behaviorism at the positivist pole, with functionalism leaning toward the positivist side of the center of the humanist-positivist continuum. The remaining theories would lie at varying points along the continuum (e.g., Homans' exchange theory lies at the positivist pole, Blau's more toward the center).

I. The old distinction between human and nonhuman study, between the "cultural" and "natural" sciences, or between "personal-social" and "material-spatial" knowledge, was made more explicit at this time. It continues until today, although not always argued as purely.

Nevertheless, as sociology became an American discipline after the First World War, it became an American "science" defined more in empiricist than in positivist terms. There was rejection of nineteenth-century progress and "evolution" views as a priori and theory spinning. Sociology turned to fact gathering to repair its empirical shortcomings, i.e., there were many "theories" but few "facts." Moreover, using social data to help solve the "social problems" that were dominant in immigrant, urbanizing, and industrializing America was seen as the major rationale for the support of sociological endeavors. Hence, the between-the-wars period (1920–40) was characterized by fervent and varying empirical sociological activity. Studies were made of families, communities (both urban and rural), social change, social psychology, crime and delinquency, deviants, population, and the like. Leaning to the scientific model that emphasized experiments, controlled field studies, and statistical treatment of data were practitioners such as Ogburn, Chapin, Bernard, and Rice. Stressing the more humanistic case study and participant observation approaches—but still "fact-oriented"—were Thomas, Park, and the Lynds, for example. Less given to a "social problems" outlook but stressing instead "bigger" societal, historical, and intellectual issues requiring rational analysis, historical reconstruction, and empathy were writers such as Vierkandt, Alfred Weber, Scheler, and Znaniecki in Europe and Elwood and MacIver in America.

Emerging out of this period was a growing sophistication of "scientific method" along positivist lines. Influenced by logical positivism in philosophy and impressed by the history and accomplishments of natural (particularly physical) science, workers such as Bain, Lundberg, and Hart emphasized objective measurement, operationism, and deductive theory. This movement was sometimes known as neo-positivism. Also concerned with social application, neo-positivists stressed that application should reflect scientific knowledge rather than fuzzy ideals or wishful thinking. Neo-positivism, appearing before World War II, became dominant after the war. Its main opposition came from European humanists such as Mannheim and Gurvitch; transplanted Europeans in America such as Wirth, Sorokin, and MacIver; and American humanists and interactionists such as Waller, H. P. Becker, and Blumer.

One attempt to bridge the continual polemics between humanists and positivists was a "theory-method" emphasis in the late 1940s. Robert Merton, its leading exponent, called for peace, dialogue, and integration between "theoretical generalizers" and "small-scale researchers" (Merton, 1949: chaps. 2 and 3). In his discussion, he delineated several ways in which each could influence the other. To some degree, declared Merton, this was already happening; it was to have some influence (cf. Westie, 1957; Schermerhorn and Boskoff, 1957:76).

It seemed manifestly reasonable that a sociological science should emphasize both theory and research, should never stress theory or method alone, and should integrate these. Such an approach would leave sociology within the scientific tradition but would moderate that tradition. It would insist on theory, but theory that was testable; it was ultimately grounded in facts. It would insist on research using scientific method, but method geared to theory.

The theory-method ideal had but limited success, however, even during its high point in the middle and late 1950s. First, it went against the empiricist tendencies of many sociologists (see chapter 1 in this volume) with their disinclination to theory and lack of methodological discipline. Second, while it moderated some "radical operationalists" at one extreme and "pure theorists" at the other, many other methodologists and theorists avoided the proposed theory-method compromise because it inhibited them from freely developing their own inclinations. Third, and most dramatic, the *moderate* scientific model for sociology implied by theory-method proponents satisfied neither humanists nor positivists, for opposite reasons. While the new humanism and neo-positivism could each still be called versions of a theory-method approach, each in its own way actually has violated the theory-method integration ideal—the "new humanism" by eschewing scientific rigor (and science altogether), the new positivism by a narrow and formalistic interpretation of science.

The temporal development of the above controversies can be shown in abridged form as follows:

Evolution of Theory-Method Issues in Sociology

1. *Nineteenth-century Imperialism*

    Hopes for science of society by St. Simone, Comte, Spencer. Overt rejection of philosophic speculation in favor of positivism in theory and method. Actually very speculative. Accompanied by some empiricism, both formal (Quetelet) and descriptive (Le-Play, Spencer, Toennies). This view not seriously challenged by American "pioneers" (e.g. Ward, Sumner).

2. *Turn-of-century Verstehen-Science Debate*
   (1890–1920)
   Reaction to Ranke historical tradition and, in sociology, to Comte and the early Durkheim by subjective idealism and ideographism of Dilthey; Weber took middle position. In the United States, Cooley and Giddings represented opposite sides of this debate.

3. *Between-the-wars Empiricism and*
   Social Problems Era (1920–35)
   American sociology to the fore, sought to build science of society via variety of data-gathering and measuring devices and to apply findings to solve social problems (Ogburn, Bernard, Rice, Gillin). Also strong positivist side in von Wiese and Chapin. Case study and life-history emphasized by Thomas, Park, Lynds. Opposing this was rational-idealist (humanist) position stressing rational analysis, historical reconstruction, and/or empathy (Vierkandt, Alfred Weber, Scheler, Znaniecki in Europe; Ellwood, MacIver in America).

4. *Neo-positivism (1935–50)*
   A growing sophistication of empiricism into the neo-positivism of Bain, Lundberg, Hart, Dodd. Stressed operationism, deductive theory, objective measurement; was related to influence of logical positivism in philosophy. Favored social application but, unlike some humanists, saw no major moral issues in this (technological view). Opposed by humanism (ra-

tional idealist) of some Europeans (e.g., Mannheim, Gurvitch), transplanted Europeans (e.g., MacIver, Znaniecki, Sorokin, Wirth), and American humanists and interactionists (e.g., Waller, Becker, Parsons, E. Faris, Blumer).

5. *Theory-method Era (1950–63)*

Reaction by early 1950s to neo-positivism's "radical operationism" and general anti-intellectualism, on the one hand, and to all-inclusive theoretical systems, on the other. Led to theory-method emphasis, some leaning more to theory (Merton, Cottrell, Homans), others more to method (Lazarsfeld, Stouffer, Guttman), some more middle-of-the-road (Bales, T. Mills, Strodtbeck, Riecken). Led to compromise, theories of the "middle range," small theories. Much was lip service to theory-method. The former rational-idealist and humanist tradition of Sorokin, MacIver, Blumer type, unlike the neo-positivists who nominally embraced theory-method, continued as a separate force, joined by others such as Timasheff, Furfey, Riesman, Coser.

6. *Present Polarized Era (1963 on)*

Theory-method consensus ignored by empiricists who dominate sociology, broken by the new humanism of the early 1960s and neo-positivism (formalism) soon after.

THE "NEW HUMANISTS"

The largest and most dramatic departure from theory-method may be called the New Sociology (Horowitz, 1964), humanistic theory (Berger, 1963; Goodwin,

1973:3–4), the humanistic rebellion, or the "underground," although a more fitting name might be the *new humanism*. The key is *involvement* in several senses of the word—theoretical, methodological, and activist. Theoretically, it stresses the humanistic subject matter of sociology, emphasizing meanings and values within complex and changing political, economic, and cultural settings that are part of an historical process (Berger, 1963; Cameron, 1963; Coser, 1963, 1972; Berger and Luckmann, 1966; Holzner, 1968 and 1972; Dreitzel, 1970; Glass and Staude, 1972; Bowman, 1973; Psathas, 1973). Methodologically, new humanists distrust the rigor of science as excessive and increasingly sterile and favor more loose-jointed methodologies—such as participant observation and phenomenological approaches —that recognize the qualitative difference between social life and other phenomena (cf. Cicourel, 1964; Bruyn, 1966; Garfinkel, 1967, Glaser and Strauss, 1967; Sjoberg and Nett, 1968; Filstead, 1970; Denzin, 1970). Finally, sociology is continually challenged to become relevant to the "human condition"—from the prosaic to the poignant, dramatic, and violent—the field becoming authentic only by so doing (cf. Mills, 1959; Stein and Vidich, 1963; Horowitz, 1964, 1967a; Sjoberg, 1967; Gouldner, 1970; Friedrichs, 1970; Lee, 1973). Thus, humanism has several meanings, not all of which are shared by all new humanists.

Characteristic of the new humanists is their rejection of the still-dominant American "social problems" perspective in favor of a "social issues" orientation. The "social problems" perspective accepted societal goals (e.g., to restore organization, to bring about orderly progress) while attempting to develop scientific *means* to cure "disorganized" conditions such as slums, crime, and divorce. In contrast, the "issues-oriented" new humanists posit a more total orientation, seeing their own role and competence to be the questioning of both goals and means of society rather than leaving these to the politician, businessman, clergy, or foundation official. The new humanists, therefore, tend to have ill-disguised disdain for the "social problems" approaches as reformist and piecemeal in an age that requires bold and dramatic approaches. (See chapter 7, pages 134–36 in this volume, for a more extended treatment.)

Illustrative of the new humanist temper, particularly its radical side, is Irving Louis Horowitz's call for a "dialectical sociology." He writes:

> What needs to be established in sociology is some recognition that the grounds of the field still rest on people no less than powers, masses no less than elites, spontaneity no less than equilibrium, revolution no less than reaction, conflict no less than consensus. (1967a: 367)

Bill Harrell, newer to sociology than Horowitz, has expressed the general sentiments of the new humanism even more clearly and forcefully:

> I am not committed to an objective science for its own sake but an objective science informed by a critical philosophy which is in turn informed by the finding of an objective science. In the last analysis, who gives a hang whether an institution is functional for society or not if it is not functional for all the men involved. Man is a social animal not for society's sake but for the animal's sake. (1967:120, note 20)

The new humanism is a free-spirited intellectual rebellion that is critical of the emphasis upon formal theory

construction and positivistic research methods. It sees
these developments as the consequence of emphasizing
the scientific vision of sociology at the expense of its
humanistic subject matter (see an earlier warning by
Burgess, 1953). The current scene is further characterized
in Sorokin-like terms as "intellectual amnesia": there is
insufficient awareness of classical sociological thought,
Marxist and other. Thus, the new humanists argue for
sociology as a scholarly and humane discipline that must
(1) utilize the work of the older masters without being
limited by their vision, (2) create further theory without
being bound by the necessity of formalizing or "verify-
ing" it, and (3) make use of a great variety of methods
for defining, gathering, measuring, interpreting, and presenting data.

Further, the "new breed" (not all of them young)
consists of people who see themselves as sensitive human
beings, observers, participants, and/or intellectuals fully
as much as sociologists—for to be the last, one must be
the others. Hence, a prime duty is to involve onself in
issues of the day—moral, political, and aesthetic. Given
this view, the new humanists continually posit for sociology the task of relevance to such issues.

Although their general political tendency has been
to the left, the new humanists are not united politically or
ideologically. What they have in common is a similar view
about the nature and goals of sociology, that is, its humanistic character and the necessity for involvement in
social action. The key, as indicated earlier, is *involvement*
—participating in the life of college fraternities and
medical students; in the efforts of the poor to organize
their slum and of inmates to cope with their "total institution"; or in a rising social movement to outlaw taxes
and preserve property values, maintain law and order,

promote black power, or demonstrate in support of, or opposition to, military spending. "Involvement" thus comes to have both methodological and activist connotations. Scientific method, even when broadly defined, is seen as but one of several legitimate methods and yields a distorted picture when used alone. Ethical neutrality is deemed impossible and/or undesirable and seen to be a sham.

There is a new feeling in the air. It is one of distrust of any overriding theoretical or methodological system, of any single ideology, of any existing political, economic, and/or religious setting. Even Marxists among the new humanists are likely to take an independent line, showing greater interest in issues than in ideology, though less inclined to reject science (cf. Szymanski, 1973). The new humanists were not satisfied with the theory-method brake (Merton, 1949) upon positivism and "scientism." While theory-method had indeed arrested some extreme tendencies and rigidities of the positivist scientific vision, it still retained a commitment to science, with its formalistic tendencies in theory and method. Instead, the new humanists made a clean break with a scientific sociology by taking different theoretical, methodological, and applied directions, usually subjectivist and sometimes irrationalist.

NEO-POSITIVIST SOCIOLOGIES

Another departure from the theory-method ideal, one propounding a narrower view of science, is neo-positivist (formalized and mathematical) sociology. The latter, less sharply outlined than the new humanism, has been growing steadily. It features mathematical and other formal models. Emphasized have been theory construction (particularly beginning in the late 1960s), formalization of variables, experimental logics, computer technologies and languages, and laboratory and computer simulation of interaction and of organizational and communication behavior (Berger et al., 1962, 1966, 1972; Fararo and Sunshine, 1964; Stinchcombe, 1968; Dubin, 1969; Blalock, 1969; Sonquist, 1970; Abell, 1971; Mullins, 1971; Reynolds, 1971; Hage, 1972; Gibbs, 1972; Willer and Willer, 1973). Used are techniques and "tools" such as set theory, causal and path analysis, latent structure analysis, game theory, graph theory, matrices and vectors, index construction, decision functions, Markov chains, and stochastic models (Coleman, 1964; McGinnis, 1965; Bartholomew, 1967 and 1974; Bartos, 1967; Galtung, 1967; Lazarsfeld and Henry, 1968; Borgatta, 1969; Borgatta and Bohrnstedt, 1970; Beauchamp, 1970; Costner, 1971, 1972, 1973; Fararo, 1973). Related to the upsurge in formalized sociology is an increase in sociology laboratory manuals and texts in methodology and statistics written specifically for sociologists. Further evidence of this trend is the rise to prominence of mathematical sociology and the formalization of theory at several graduate centers.

The above continues the long "natural science" tradition that stems from Bacon's empiricist (and interventionist) hopes for a social science; the naturalism of Galileo and Newton; the incipient positivism of Hume; the strong empiricism and later positivism of Mach and Pearson; the "conventionalism" of Poincaré; and twentieth-century movements in analytic philosophy, logical positivism, and operationalism. In sociology itself, neopositivism is faithful to traditions running from Comte to Lundberg (see pages 80–82 in this chapter) and is continuous with the scientific methodology of workers in the post-World War II period such as Stouffer, Lazarsfeld, and Guttman. Like their intellectual ancestors, current formalistic and mathematical sociologists take it for granted that sound scientific methodology, which includes theory formalization, is the first principle of sociology. Sociological analysis must fit the scientific canons that will, or promise to, achieve validity and reliability, particularly the latter. To bring this about, models and techniques that enable the formulation and testing of theories —usually resembling those of the more successful physical and behavioral sciences—are emphasized and developed. Often, there is strong influence from methodological developments in behavioral science disciplines such as economics, business organization, and experimental psychology.

That formalistic and mathematical sociologists are positivistic (rather than, say, empiricist, idealist, or rationalist) can be seen in (1) their emphasis upon "observable" data, including a wary view toward causation (cf. Gibbs, 1972a); (2) their use of formal devices to relate "unobservable" terms to experience deductively; (3) their ready willingness to treat "empirically observable wholes" in terms of "constructs" that break the wholes into more "handleable" parts; (4) their working assumption that science cannot deal directly with reality —and that the only alternative is to treat much of conceptual phenomena as "constructs" and as nominal and operational definitions; and (5) the relative simplicity, circumspection, and intellectual conservatism of their work.

Nor is neo-positivism confined to pure or abstract sociology. It has developed in applied directions as well. Thus, neo-positivism has been applied to problems in areas such as population by, for example, Hauser and

Duncan; to business organization by Dubin and Lazarsfeld; to education by Coleman; and to prediction of delinquency by Monachesi and Schrag. Further, emphasis is often on practical considerations in theory construction and research as well as on the more formalistic ones.[2]

Though less dramatic than the new humanism, mathematical and formalized sociology (neo-positivism) has been at least as persistent and perhaps more stable and consistent in its growth. It is not anti-theory for it features theory logic, construction, and testing. Hence, its strong methodological emphasis should not be seen as a methodological determinism (i.e., that theory should adjust to method). A more fair characterization might be *formalistic determinism,* i.e., forcing both theory and method into a limited range of formal models. Positivistic in tone and leaning toward "physicalist" variables (e.g., Catton, 1966; Park, 1969), it extends and refines the already dominant scientific mathematical methodology as preferred, if not necessary, for sociology (cf. Costner and Blalock, 1972:834), a more restricted conception of science than Merton had in mind.

CONCLUSIONS

There is some question, as sociology moves through the 1970s, whether the present humanist-positivist polarization will continue or whether the new humanism will

2. For example, Clarence Schrag, a criminologist and former Lundberg student, argues that it is difficult to satisfy all four criteria for theoretical adequacy, i.e., logical, operational, empirical, and pragmatic. One must decide which criteria to emphasize and which to slight, depending on the relative emphasis upon goals such as prediction, social control, generality, testability, consistency, and the like (1967:250–52).

decline to the minority role that humanistic sociology usually has held.[3] There appears to be little question that neo-positivism, formalization, and mathematical sociology are growing. Books continue to be published that feature both old and new quantitative techniques and that are geared to a computer technology (Borgatta and Bohrnstedt, 1970; Beauchamp, 1970; Reynolds, 1971; Blalock, 1971; Costner, 1972, 1973; Hage, 1972; Gibbs, 1972b; Fararo, 1973). Moreover, national and regional conventions continue to feature sessions on topics such as mathematical sociology, model building, and theory construction, some of these under the theory label. Neo-positivist sociology seems very likely to survive, receiving support from the traditional view of sociology as a natural science, from the demands of an industrial technology, and from neo-positivist influence over professional associations and journals.

New humanist sociologists also continue to have an impact, as judged by new college courses with their associated readings; texts with a "qualitative" and "soft" methodology focus (cf. Denzin, 1970; Filstead, 1970; Lofland, 1971; Psathas, 1973); and the "opening up" of sociology conventions to humanist, radical, and "activist" sessions devoted to women, the poor, and black and other ethnic minorities.[4] Nevertheless, while nonradical hu-

3. There have been recent signs of counterattack, not only by neo-positivists, against humanistic theory and method (cf. Demerath, 1970; Horton and Bouma, 1970–1971; Catton, 1971, 1972; Lidz, 1972; Nettler, 1972).

4. The 1970, 1971, 1972, and 1973 American Sociological Association conventions have seen 14 sessions wholly devoted to "humanist" topics (such as humanistic sociology, phenomenological sociology, and ethnomethodology) or 1, 5, 4, and 4 for the four years, respectively—whereas there were 30 sessions devoted to "neo-positivist" topics (such as measurement, mathematical sociology, models, and theory construction)—or 5, 3, 17, and 5 for the four years. In addition, many other sessions had single papers that could fit one of

manists (e.g., interactionists, phenomenologists, ethnomethodologists, reality constructionists) have been pene-
trating the major sociological journals and have been
prolific publishers of books, this has not been the case for
radical and Marxist sociologists. They have largely had to
confine their efforts to books, to pamphlets, and to radical
and Marxist journals (cf. Collins, 1972–73), some outside of sociology and the social sciences (e.g., *Monthly
Review, Radical America, Socialist Revolution*), others
within (e.g., *Society, Catalyst, Telos, Insurgent Sociologist*). Humanist sociology seems likely to survive, perhaps
as an effective minority, both because of traditional humanist views about human behavior and because of the
continuing strength of radical and Marxist sociology in
Europe and America.

Whether the indefinite future be a continuing positivist-humanist polarization or the triumph of either neo-
positivism or humanism, the near future at least promises
to be intellectually and morally stimulating and intolerant.
Stimulation will be guaranteed as long as both positivists
and humanists remain strong. Intolerance, intellectual
and moral, is inevitable whether or not the polarization
continues, that intolerance becoming particularly suf-
focating were one side or the other to triumph, since its
theory-method and value ideology (that is to be taken for
granted) would then permeate all sociology. It is for-
tunate, therefore, that the majority of sociologists follows
the field's more limited, and less stimulating, interests and
remains apart from the positivist-humanist controversy.

---

the above classifications. Also, one can raise the above totals by add-
ing sessions devoted to radical, activist, and "underdog" orientations
to the humanist totals and sessions in demography, ecology, small
groups, and organizations to the positivist totals. Finally, the above
figures should be seen relative to the *total* number of sessions at each
convention (92 in 1970, 142 in 1971, 179 in 1972, 170 in 1973).

The next two chapters deal with logical issues of theory and its testing. Chapter 5 finds surprising near-unanimity about the question of a single theory in sociology and sees this as a case of "sociological lag." Chapter 6 notes less uniformity around the question of a single structure or form for theories and the question of a single method for all sociology. Both chapters, particularly the latter, are informed by the continuing humanist-positivist confrontation.

5 *"Sociological Lag":*
Single Theory Advocates and Critics

The present chapter deals with arguments for and against a single theory in sociology. As was the case before the 1960s, single theory advocacy is widely shared and includes positivists, humanists, and those holding more moderate views toward science—functionalists, for example. So dominant is the single theory position in sociology that, except for a few "shaky" examples, one needs to go outside sociology to find multiple theory exponents. That one must go to other behavioral and even natural sciences to find questioning of, and even challenges to, the single theory ideal indicates an "intellectual lag" in sociology.

THE QUESTION OF A SINGLE THEORY

Single Theory Advocates

Those inclining to a single theory tend to take at least one of the following positions. The first is to deny the existence of theories competing with their own (Parsons, for example). A second is to define their discipline in terms of their theory (e.g., Davis, 1959; Lundberg, 1939:pt. 1, or 1964). A third is to see their own theory as the only legitimate one while recognizing the existence and influence of competing theories, as in the case of Homans (1964a and 1964b), Blumer (1956, 1962, and 1966a), and Gurvitch (Bosserman, 1968). A fourth position is to point to a growing convergence of sociology toward their own theory (e.g., Parsons, 1961a, 1970; Lundberg, 1956, 1964:Epiloque; Martindale, 1960:541; Gurvitch, in Bosserman, 1968; Sorokin, 1966:chap. 18; Timasheff, 1967:chap. 2). A fifth and last position is to favor the throwing out of all existing "theory" as being of little or no value and starting anew (as in the case of Berger, Zelditch, and Anderson, 1966, 1972).

Talcott Parsons, relatively modest in his early work (1937), came to refer to his progressing work as the only sociological theory extant. His self-conscious movement toward a general theory became evident with the emergence of his "structure-function" approach (1945, 1951), particularly his collaboration with other social and behavioral scientists around an "action frame of reference" (Parsons and Shils, 1951). However, this was still but a "major movement" that "helped to deepen the channel of the [social science] river" (1951:viii) but was not yet, presumably, the river itself.[1] By the late 1950s and continuing thereafter, Parsons' writings were arguing for theory integration across disciplines (1959b:36–37, 1966:v) and assuming or implying that his theory was the road to general theory in sociology (1961a:30–33, 1970:28–29, 60–61). Wilbert Moore, applying a modified functionalism to social change, lends support to this in stating that most social science disciplines consist of structural-functional analysis (1960:817).

An even more extreme functionalist reaction was presented by Kingsley Davis. In his 1959 American Sociological Association presidential address, Davis argued that all sociological theory is functionalism, and vice versa. Since every science describes and explains phenomena from the standpoint of a *system* of reasoning which presumably bears a relation to a corresponding *system* in nature, then the fact that we are scientists makes us functionalists, and vice versa. All sociologists relate parts (data) to the whole (theory system) and one part to another (data to data) (1959:758–59).[2] In so arguing, not only does Davis assume one theory-method for sociology—the main point at issue here—but he also appears to confuse two things: (1) a philosophic commitment to a deductive model of theory, i.e., a hierarchical-axiom-type logical structure[3] that incorporates empirical generalizations with (2) a substantive sociological commitment to functionalism, i.e., the wholistic assumption

1. The same volume was less uncertain about a preferred *form* for conceptual schemes in all scientific disciplines, offering four "levels" of systematization (Parsons and Shils, 1951:50–51).

2. Marion Levy, another "structural functionalist," agrees (1968:22).

3. See chapter 6, pages 109–15, in this volume for discussion of the hierarchical theory model.

that the whole is prior to the parts (cf. Martindale, 1960: 447).

Even Robert Merton, who advised against "the quest for an all-embracing unified theory" as premature (1968: 45), did not give up the goal of a unified theory. His urging that sociologists pursue "middle range" theories (1949:5–10, 1968:chap. 2) was advice for the present and for the foreseeable future. The single general theory ideal remained.

The functionalist inclinations to one theory are paralleled just as strongly by "neo-positivists" such as Lundberg and Homans. George Lundberg, in the epilogue to a revised and abridged edition of his 1939 classic, *Foundations of Sociology,* argued that not only had sociologists as dissimilar as Talcott Parsons and Robert Bales converged by the early 1950s—a widely noticed event—but their work is really parallel to that of Stuart Dodd's since 1947 (Lundberg, 1964:167–68, originally in Lundberg, 1956:22–23). In effect, Lundberg was saying that the Parsons of 1937, who had excoriated positivism for many pages, had come around to the positivist, neo-positivist, or "natural science" position of Lundberg, Dodd, and Bales by the early 1950s (i.e., Parsons and Shils, 1951; Parsons, Bales, and Shils, 1953). Parsons realized that his motivational paradigm and pattern variables were conceptualizing the same thing referred to by Bales' categories of "interaction process analysis," both writers being particularly concerned with the "functional problems of social systems." Even more significant to Parsons' convergence with a natural science conclusion is Parsons' convergence with Dodd; Parsons' actors, situation, and orientation comparing to Dodd's people, time-space-residual factors, and actions and values. Finally, Lundberg compares Bales' twelve interaction categories with an adapted version of Dodd's and finds them similar (1964:170, 1956:26).

George Homans also argues for one type of theory in sociology: psychological theory. In an article evaluating contemporary theory (1964b), psychological theory is contrasted with two sociological theories, structural and functional. In his 1964 American Sociological Association presidential address, on the other hand, modern sociology has been reduced to one theory, i.e., only "structural-functionalism, or functionalism for short . . . has been the dominant, indeed the only distinct, school of sociological thought" (1964a:809). Some of Homans' later writing (1967a, 1969) repeats the earlier arguments more concisely. In then arguing for the reducibility of functionalism (the only sociological school) to psychological theory, Homans proposed to replace one monolith with another.

Herbert Blumer, a critic of both functionalism (1962:186) and of the general theory and method approach of "neo-positivists" or "natural scientists" (1966b), has long argued for the greater veridicality of his own conceptual approach. Blumer (some of whose basic symbolic interactionist ideas are discussed in chapter 2, page 30, of this volume) offers his interpretation of George H. Mead's "social behaviorism" as a more accurate view of actual social interaction than those posited by behaviorists, functionalists, and exponents of cultural and structural explanations (cf. 1962, 1966a, 1966b, 1969). Other interactionists have tended to share Blumer's single theory views (cf. Rose, 1962:chap. 1; Kuhn, 1964:79; Stone and Farberman, 1970:Introduction; Klapp, 1973:xiii, 302–5).

A further source of support for a single theory in

sociology had long been presented by late European and European-trained "humanists" such as Gurvitch, Sorokin, and Timasheff. Georges Gurvitch contended that the integration and advance of sociology can be arrived at in but one way, i.e., by using his method, "depth sociology." This, a vertical approach to the study of "total social phenomena," has ten levels, beginning with "the surface level of morphology and ecology," at the top, and running to "the collective mind," the tenth level, at the bottom (Bosserman, 1968:110–40); the intermediate levels include social organization, social patterns, unorganized collective behavior, and social symbols. Finally, the method of depth sociology must renounce any particular philosophical thesis or orientation (Bosserman, 1968: 106–7).

Pitirim Sorokin, sympathetic with much of Gurvitch's work, began his revised theory text (1966) by deploring the previous forty years (that is, 1925 through 1965) of "analytical sociology." This era, and kind of sociology, had been dominated by empirical, technique-oriented, micro-sociology, on the one hand; and empty, ghostly, macro-sociology systems and models, on the other. These styles of sociology lean to mechanistic analogies of equilibrium, inertia, thermodynamic laws, and system-maintenance. Instead of analytic sociology, Sorokin hopefully anticipated an emerging "synthetic" stage comparable to the pre-1925 period (exemplified by Tarde, Durkheim, Weber, Pareto, Ward, Sumner). The new "synthetic" era would be based on the convergence of most past and present theories "toward a set of principles and propositions acceptable to all" (1966: 635) and represented by Sorokin's own "integral" theory (see chapter 2 in this volume).

Another older humanist and Sorokin admirer and confidant, Nicholas Timasheff, concluded well over a decade ago (1957:chap. 22)—and again more recently (1967:chap. 22)—that modern sociology has come to accept "several positive results." He presented several of these as a basis for agreement among most sociologists, with four (dealing with basic units, processes, culture, and change) forming the groundwork for a future general theory (1967:317).

Critics of all existing theory are Berger, Zelditch, and Anderson (1966, 1972), exponents of a formalistic and mathematical sociology who press for a new beginning in theory. They complain that modern theory books are *about,* rather than *of,* theory, and usually are organized around prominent names, major schools, or major perspectives (1966:ix) and that current theory is more historically oriented than generalizing (1972:xix–xxi). Thus, students of sociological theory have available to them few, if any, compilations of "essential case materials on systematic theory" equivalent to inventories of research models available to students of methodology (1966:x). Hence, Berger et al. offer their collections as the first two in a series of volumes containing examples of systematic theory construction and generalizing research. The objectives of volume 1 are: (1) to attempt abstract, general formulations; (2) to make these as explicit and logically tight as possible so as to expose hidden assumptions; and (3) to subject these to empirical test (1966: xi–xii). The articles cover a variety of subjects under the categories of "social interaction" and "social structure," the editors stating that most of the theories are seen by the contributing authors as tentative beginnings that require (more) empirical testing. Volume 2 (1972) offers articles on topics such as exchange, authority, and status structures within the overall objective of contributing to generalizing knowledge in sociology.

Multiple Theory Advocates

While single theory advocates, self-conscious and implied, abound in sociology, one has to search extensively to find self-conscious multiple theory advocates. Usually this involves some intellectual stretching, as in the cases discussed later where the argument is made for several coexisting theoretical perspectives. One possible example was Robert Bierstedt's "theoretic bias" prescription in the early 1960s. Bierstedt saw sociology as too narrow in its predilection for scientific method and called for it to be a humane discipline as well (1960). In following the latter course, he asked that more sociologists utilize "the theoretic bias," an approach that would push and exaggerate particular interpretations of social phenomena for heuristic purposes (as Marx, Buckle, and Weber did), trusting for a dialectic process to refine, modify, and correct these (1960:8). While the dialectic process suggests an eventual "synthesis" of interpretation, it also implies that multiple interpretations will continue to arise and compete.

A more circumscribed example of advocacy of coexisting theories is the attempt to use both consensus (or order) theories and conflict theories as necessary to treat all of social relations. Thus (as already developed in chapter 3, pages 60–62, in this volume), writers such as Dahrendorf, Horowitz, Ossowski, and Lenski see empirical bases for two theories: consensus theories for some aspects of social life (or to some kinds of society) and conflict theories for others.

Self-conscious multiple theory advocates in sociology thus are almost nonexistent.[4] Their number would increase if one counted what sociologists actually do in practice, that is, they use one theory for one problem or kind of data and a second theory for another problem or kind of data. Perhaps one can also include Merton if one ignores his acceptance of a total theory system for the distant future and pays more attention to his current plea for several theories of the middle range (1949:5–10; 1968:chap. 2). Similarly, Walter Wallace maintains what he characterizes "as an ultimately vain but irresistible search for a single general theory" (1969:59), vain because such a theory would need to incorporate a number of dimensions that appear difficult to integrate, e.g., objective and subjective, social genesis and social maintenance (1969:pt. 1). One could therefore count Merton and Wallace as single theory advocates in principle but multiple theory advocates in practice.

To find more proponents of multiple theories in a discipline, one needs to go outside sociology. For example, the contention has been made in a recent social psychology theories text that social psychology "is too diverse a

4. Ferdinand (1969) proposed the impossibility of a general theory of behavior, arguing that it is impossible to integrate the social sciences with, say, psychology or physiology. Since these "unique" disciplines are on different levels, say, sociology (e.g., social role) and psychology (e.g., personality), any statements linking sociological concepts with psychological concepts violate Bertrand Russell's vicious circle principle that "no statement can define a concept that also includes the statement itself" (1969:331). Ferdinand also refers to Goedel's proof to argue against a complete theory of behavior. However, he does not appear to deny the possibility of a general theory for one discipline where the question of levels is not involved (see also Bradley and Reynolds, 1970, and Gray, 1972, for criticisms of Ferdinand's logical arguments and of his conclusion about a general theory of behavior).

group of relatively young subdisciplines to be accounted for by any single network of hypotheses" (Shaw and Costanzo, 1970:363). The authors of the only other social psychology text completely devoted to theories have written: "Nowadays it is recognized increasingly that human action must be seen from various perspectives if its many facets are to be understood (Deutsch and Krauss, 1965:215). These authors argue that there is no one sovereign explanation because of "human complexity" and criticize the "outdated and grandiose notion that there can be one general theory," calling this notion a prejudice. After all, "physics has a muddle of theories. There is need in social psychology for a variety of conceptual frames and theories to embrace the richness of human behavior" (1965:215).

This point was underscored by a psychologist, Sigmund Koch, and a philosopher of science, Michael Scriven (see Wann, 1964). Critical of continuing attempts by other psychologists to define their field in unitary terms as the science of *behavior,* Koch contends that no other science does this. For example, physics is divided into optical, mechanical, magnetic, and intra-atomic events; biology into metabolism, growth, reproduction, contraction, and secretion—each subarea having its own laws rather than a single set of laws for physics or biology as a whole. Koch calls the tendency toward one definition and one system of laws for an entire discipline (psychology) "S-R scholasticism" and blames such a view largely on the emphasis by logical positivism and analytic philosophy upon an "age of theory" that seeks one unified big theory for all (1964:33–34).

Also using physics as an example of variety in theory, Scriven wrote the following:

Nobody can relate quantum field theory to general field theory. Nobody knows what to do with particle theory. Nobody knows how to handle the behavior of liquid helium . . . the plasma field is just beginning. We have local theories for each subject. . . . There is not an over-arching synthesis. (1964:188–89)

At another place in his article, Scriven decried the "tendency . . . to extend a useful explanatory theory into other realms, where its value is non-existent except in making the smell of the account attractive to other users of this scent" (1964:176).

A theoretical physicist, Richard Feynman, has been quoted by Robert Merton to support many of these sentiments. Arguing in the same vein as Koch and Scriven, Feynman has written that theories and laws of physics "are a multitude of different parts and pieces that do not fit together very well" (1965:30, quoted in Merton, 1967:48 and 1968:48).

CONCLUSIONS

In sociology, the advocacy and/or hope for a single, general, unified (integrated) theory is not merely dominant, it is nearly unanimous. In other behavioral sciences and in the natural sciences, such advocacy is less monolithic. Yet, except when a discipline actually succeeds in forging a single theory that incorporates all its knowledge, the belief in a single theory remains a rationalistic, extra-scientific bias, one outstanding example of this being Albert Einstein's persisting search for a unified physical theory in the last part of his life (Merton, 1967:48 or 1968:48).

Perhaps a single, general theory will emerge, though that might require the creativity of two or more cooperating Einsteins. Several obstacles seem to stand in the way. One is the practical problem for a general theory to incorporate the many narrower theories and empirical findings—perhaps an insuperable task. More basic may be the diversity of a field's subject matter (apparently as true in physics as in sociology), with its corresponding methodological diversity. Finally, there might be innate or societal limitations to human abstracting and generalizing abilities. Therefore, the hope for a general theory remains a hope—even a wish—unfortunately expressed as an imperative to more modest sociologists working on more narrow, concrete problems. Rather than trying to create guilt-ridden anxiety for others, it would be better for single theory advocates to leave others alone until they themselves are closer to realizing their dream.

This chapter has indicated that a small minority of theorists advocates several coexisting theories, either giving an empirical basis for this (e.g., Dahrendorf, Deutsch and Krauss, Koch) or practical reasons (e.g., Shaw and Costanzo, Scriven, Feynman). That sociologists are relatively absent from the multiple theory camp is surprising in view of the heterogeneity of their subject matter. As indicated at the beginning of this chapter, the fact that sociologists appear to be more loyal to the single, general, and integrated theory ideal than even physical scientists are may well be an "intellectual (or sociological) lag."

6 The Appropriate
Theory Structure and Method

While neo-positivists, structure functionalists, humanists, and interactionists all seem to favor a single, general, integrated theory in sociology, this near-unanimity disappears when it comes to (1) the question of a single structure or form for theory and (2) the issue of a single method for sociology. Neo-positivists, who advocate a "natural science" of sociology patterned after physics (Lundberg, 1955, 1964; Catton, 1966; Park, 1969), as well as structure functionalists, who stress a "social science" patterned after biology (Merton, 1949:

chap. 1; Aberle et al., 1950; Parsons, 1951, 1966; Levy, 1952), agree that the proper structure for theory is deductive or axiomatic and that the proper method for all empirical disciplines is the scientific method. In contrast, humanists and interactionists are much more likely to criticize the deductive structure or form for theory and also to argue for multiple methodologies.

The discussion that follows calls for alternatives to deductive theory and to a single method. It favors pragmatism—situational variation—in theory structure and in method. It does not espouse either the dismissal of deductive procedures or the overthrow of scientific method; nor does it call for their replacement by other ideals or forms. True, a new and dominant theory model or scholarly method might invigorate the field but it would probably come to exhibit the narrowness and intolerance of the model or method replaced. The call here is therefore not for a process whereby an antithesis, or even a new synthesis, comes to dominate the field but for variety in theory structure and in methods.

THE QUESTION OF A SINGLE STRUCTURE FOR THEORY

Science, like social life in general, is prone to idealization. In social life, a useful or successful practice may be copied to the degree that it becomes a folkway, an ideal, perhaps eventually even sacred. So science sometimes comes to treat a model, a method, or a paradigm as an ideal norm for all to follow. One of these is the *deductive* model for theory. The following discussion, while not espousing the dismissal of *deductive* or *axiomatic* practices, and mindful of their many advantages, seeks to place them in perspective by criticism and by examination of alternatives.

The Deductive Model

The "deductive" model as the proper one for theory is an assumption long held by many sociologists. The inclination to formal or rational procedures has a long history in Western civilization. Its basis lies in the Socratic method and in Aristotle's logic of classes (Martindale, 1960:7–9, 537–39). Despite later criticisms and modifications in logic and mathematics, the predilection for formal-hierarchical reasoning continued within science and outside, as witness the examples of Galileo and Descartes, respectively. Twentieth-century developments in analytic philosophy, symbolic logic, and the like in Europe furthered the use of formal analyses in science, as in the work of Russell, Wittgenstein, Schlick, and Carnap. This model of reasoning came to be applied not only to scientific methodology but also to the form of theory, to the logic of theory construction. Most recent texts in the philosophy and logic of science and social science and in methods of social science appear to assume the deductive model of theory and of explanation (cf. Nagel, 1961:90–97; Brown, 1963:chap. 11; McEwen, 1963; Scheffler, 1963:7–15; Brodbeck, 1968: Introduction, chap. 21).

In sociology, deductive theory has been very influential (Ward, 1974:34, 36). The foremost exponents of the deductive or axiomatic models have been not only "neo-positivists" and mathematical sociologists (cf. Lundberg, 1939:pt. 1; Zetterberg, 1954; Coleman, 1964; Galtung, 1967; Homans, 1967b; Stinchcombe, 1968; Blalock, 1969; Wallace, 1971), but also structure-functionalists (cf. Parsons, 1937:7–9; Merton, 1949:96–99; Parsons and Shils, 1951:50–51; Levy, 1952, 1963;

Smelser, 1968:6). Even some humanist and interactionist sociologists appeared to accept it (cf. Rose, 1954:chap. 1, 1962: chap. 1; Kinch, 1963; Timasheff, 1967:10), though, as we shall see, this is not true for all of them.

Criticisms of the Deductive Ideal

The 1960s and even earlier periods included negative reactions to the deductive model in sociology and related disciplines. For example, Barrington Moore criticized structure-functionalist promulgation of deductive theory as "neo-scholasticism" largely because the abstract categories and formal manipulations suggest much but deliver little (1958:97–100). Another critic, Dennis Wrong, saw Parsons' acceptance of the view that "sociological theory should strive to imitate the logical structure and degree of abstraction of theoretical physics. . . ." as ill advised (Wrong, 1963:316). The more productive sociologists (such as Marx, Weber, Cooley, Mannheim) did not first check with philosophers of science; instead, their sociology was a byproduct of their seeking answers to substantive problems (Wrong, 1963: 317). Glaser and Strauss (1967) criticize theory formalizers for not sufficiently grounding their formal theory in more substantive theories in several different subject areas (1967:chap. 4), the formalizers often playing "theoretical capitalists" who expect "proletariat testers" to do the actual testing of hypotheses derived from their (the "capitalists'") theories (1967:10–11). Melvin Marx, in his preface to an early 1960s reader in psychological theory, sees a "drastic decline in interest [between 1951 and 1963] in highly formalized theory, particularly of the Hullian hypothetico-deductive variety" (1963:v). Recognized now as "premature and overambitious," hypothetico-deductive theories have given way to the more

> spectacular . . . mathematical-type model . . . and the
> less spectacular, but perhaps more important in the long
> run . . . functional type of theory . . . closely tied
> to empirical footings and . . . designed to be devel-
> oped gradually. . . . (Marx, 1963:v)

Among the strongest critics of a single (deductive)
model for the form of a theory is Maurice Natanson
(1963), an existential and phenomenological philosopher
and close student of the social sciences. He asks that
social scientists be more self-critical, theoretical, and
philosophically literate in their conception of theory and
calls upon them to examine the "world view" underlying
their arguments about theory and methodology (1963:
14–19). For example, tending toward the deductive
model is an "objective" world view that, following a naturalistic conception of consciousness, places the individual in the context of all natural phenomena. Tending away
from the deductive model, and from modern science as
usually understood, is a "subjective" world view that, following a phenomenological approach to social reality,
sees natural science as but one aspect of the intersubjective world produced by the activity of consciousness.
Natanson clearly prefers the second, particularly with its
emphasis on "pre- or proto-empirical experience . . .
immediately experienced by the individual" (1963:15).

A more evenhanded philosophic treatment, and
one that at least accepts two models for the structure of
theory, is that of Abraham Kaplan (1964), a pragmatic
philosopher and student of the social sciences.[1] Kaplan's
work on scientific inquiry has a more "liberal" and in-
clusive view of theory, explanation, law, and fact than is

    1. An earlier work by Kaplan (and Lasswell) was one of the
targets of Barrington Moore's criticisms of deductive theory (Moore,
1958:97–99).

usually found in such books. Two models of theory structure are presented, the *hierarchical* (deductive or axiomatic type) and the *concatenated* (pattern type). The hierarchical is one

> whose component laws are presented as deductions from a small set of basic principles. A law is explained by the demonstration that it is a logical consequence of these principles, and a fact is explained when it is shown to follow from these together with certain initial conditions. (1964:298)

This follows Norman Campbell's principle that explanation is the referring of the particular to the general (1952: 79).

Kaplan contrasted the hierarchical model with the concatenated one, the latter reflecting what most sociologists (and other scientists) actually do.[2] The *concatenated* model is one

> whose component laws enter into a network of relations so as to constitute an identifiable configuration or pattern . . . [usually] converging on some central point, each specifying one of the factors which plays a part in the phenomena which the theory is to explain. (1964:298)

Explanation within this model

> may be said to be a concatenated description. It does its work not by invoking something beyond what might

2. Emphasis on what researchers "actually do," rather than on a scientific norm for research, has been more recently proposed by a philosopher and political scientist, Paul Diesing (1971:chap. 25), such an approach frequently eliciting reactions of amazement by scientists and criticized as being without standards (Diesing, 1971:319).

be described, but by putting one fact or law into relation with others. Because of the concatenation, each element of what is being described shines . . . with light reflected from all the others; it is because they come to a common focus that they throw light on what is being explained. (1964:329)

Kaplan thus offers two models of what theory, explanation, and even method are like. The hierarchical model sees explanation as logical subsuming of the specific under the general; the concatenated model stresses explanation as intelligible or meaningful relation or correlation on the same level. The author sees this distinction as widespread, referring to Gibson's contrast between *law* and *factor* types and to Einstein's *principle* (analytic) and *constructive* (synthetic) differentiation (Kaplan, 1964:298–99). Moreover, the above two models divide many leading theories between them, the hierarchical (deductive) model fitting the theories of relativity, Mendelian genetics, and Keynesian economics; and the concatenated (pattern) model fitting evolution, the "big bang" theory of cosmology, and psychoanalysis. Einstein argued that most scientific work follows the constructive (concatenated or pattern) model. Kaplan agrees, stating that while the latter model is the one most frequently used ("logic-in-use"), many scientists idealize their work ex post facto into the framework of the hierarchical or deductive ("reconstructed logic") (1964: passim).

The present discussion, in arguing against a single (deductive) ideal for the form of theory and explanation, joins a long list of suspicious interactionists, humanists, radicals, and just plain pragmatists. They are tired of the prevailing view that only one proper form for theory exists, a view presented in most methods and philosophy of science texts, in graduate courses, and at professional conferences. This almost monolithic view is proffered not only by mathematical, formalistic, and neo-positivist sociologists but by many others as well—functionalists, for example. Also, the critics are not proposing a second model or ideal, "concatenated" or other, as a substitute or even as an alternative. Rather, they advocate the idea that it is better to wear theory models loosely.[3] It is better for the form of theory to adjust to the substantive problem under study and to the nature and condition of the data —rather than to have the latter adjust to a preconceived theory form. Thus, the argument here is not against pre-conceptions, or even against the use of models or ideals as such. It is against the use of models and ideals as sacred straitjackets rather than as merely *possible* aids and guides to theoretical activity.

THE QUESTION OF A SINGLE METHOD FOR SOCIOLOGY

The Single Method Ideal

As with the arguments for a single general theory (in chapter 5) and for a deductive form for all theories (earlier in this chapter), arguments for a single method for sociology predominate over multiple method arguments. By the 1950s, the majority of sociologists appears to have accepted the idea of a single method—i.e., a single logic for research—though techniques could vary. While inheritors of the "natural science" and positivist

3. ". . . any a priori decision as to the specific type of logical system appropriate for the analysis of the social world is a decision that arbitrarily imposes a structure upon that world" (Gray, 1972:6).

tradition held this most strongly, the view was also held by "social science" advocates such as functionalists and users of smaller (less general) theories. Even interactionists, suspicious of "scientific method," offered a competing monolith by proposing their own method as best for sociology. In the 1960s, most sociologists continued to support the single method idea, at least in the absence of a conceivable alternative; but challenges to this— never wholly absent—began to be verbalized.

Perhaps the most strongly articulated arguments for a single scientific method is the "unified science" view of logical positivism (e.g., Schlick, Carnap, Reichenbach, Hempel, Feigl). The post-World War II rise of logical positivism (sometimes called logical or scientific empiricism) to a dominant position, at least in the behavioral sciences, emphasized a single method for all disciplines aspiring to "cognitive" knowledge, although granting a limited diversity to technique. Particularly in the 1950s, this idea was influential in psychology and economics and was becoming influential in sociology (e.g., Lundberg, Guttman, Homans, Zetterberg). Many sociologists gave this view at least lip service, whether or not their own work exemplified such a method.

In sociology, the neo-positivist position about science and method was most eloquently stated by George Lundberg, especially in his 1939 criticism of a distinction made by Robert MacIver. MacIver had written that

> [t]here is an essential difference, from the standpoint of causation, between a paper flying before the wind and a man flying from a pursuing crowd. The paper knows no fear and the wind no hate, but without fear and hate the man would not fly nor the crowd pursue. (MacIver, 1937:476–77, quoted in Lundberg, 1939:12)

Lundberg, calling the use of "fear" and "hate" metaphysical and animistic, said that MacIver is entitled to his distinction but

> I merely point out that possibly I could analyze the situation in a frame of reference not involving the words "fear" or "hate" but in operationally defined terms of such character that all qualified observers would independently make the same analysis and predict the behavior under the given circumstances. . . . [After all] the principle of parsimony requires that we seek to bring into the same framework the explanation of all flying objects. (1939:13)

The principles of a neo-positivist methodology for sociology have more recently been presented by Lundberg and by William Catton, a former Lundberg student. Referring to the growing trend toward "natural science," Lundberg (1955, 1964:Epilogue) saw that trend to involve (1) accepting the theory and methods of natural science; (2) accepting, therefore, operational definition and quantification as applicable to all sociology (the degree of these depending on the problem); and (3) recognizing *predictability* to be the criterion of scientific work, all techniques being judged in terms of their efficiency relative to this criterion. Therefore, it is nonsense (1) to reject these theories, methods, and techniques merely because physics has used them successfully; or (2) to accuse them of neglecting "primitive," "literary," or "psychic" concepts and variables. Similarly, Catton (1966), rejecting "animism" in favor of "naturalism," saw the latter to involve four elements: (1) asking questions capable of sensory observation in an intersubjective sense; (2) explaining phenomena in terms of antecedent and concomitant conditions—thus using efficient causes instead of functional and teleological explanation; (3) considering change, rather than continuity, to be the problem requiring explanation, with inertia deemed sufficient to account for continuity; and (4) accounting for change by change, not by unchanging factors or "unmoved movers" (1966:6–19). Lundberg and Catton have not been alone; their position has received additional support (cf. Zetterberg, 1965; Homans, 1967b; Blalock, 1969).

Functionalists, stressing variation in technique within a common scientific method, have given verbal allegiance to the single method principle. Parsons has accepted that idea for over three decades (cf. Parsons, 1937:chap. 1; Parsons and Shils, 1951:30–47, passim) as have Wilbert Moore (1963:30) and Levy (1963). Although Merton was tolerant of some variety in theory, this was not true for his view of methodology. The latter was defined as "the logic of scientific procedure" and assumed to be "common to all scientific procedure" (1949:86), that is, to all empirical disciplines; the later revisions of Merton's work did not change that view (1957:86; 1968:140). Even some admirers of the "classic" tradition seemed to accept this definition of method. For example, Schermerhorn and Boskoff defended the study of sociology's past by historians of sociology so that they might discover the relevance of the past to the "advance of science today" (1957:76). Yet, while the historian should be sensitive to the fact that "certain areas of specialization have peculiar methodological problems," still

> he must not . . . allow them the right to declare total independence of the logic of science. He must be non-partisan enough to make it clear that the *logical*

character of the natural and social sciences is not different, however the applicability of method and technique might be. (Schermerhorn and Boskoff, 1957:76)

Even a few of the more humanistic sociologists supported a single method. Some, like Roscoe and Gisela Hinkle, assumed that sociologists should use "methods patterned after other social and natural sciences, at least implicitly" (1954:73). Others, like Herbert Blumer, rejected "scientific method" in favor of a single, more "subjective" method (or technique) compatible with their own theory or view of sociology (cf. Blumer, 1956, 1962: 188–89, 1969; Bruyn, 1966; Denzin, 1970; Phillips, 1973:chap. 9). But, at least, Blumer and the others recognize multiple methodology across the sciences.

Questioning a Single Method

Yet, the very existence of a single method for all "sciences"—as well as the question that asks whether one can fruitfully distinguish between method and technique —is exactly what is in dispute, today as in the past. Max Weber early argued that a given method should be problematic and considered with, and vary according to, the problem and circumstances, a set method being "no more the precondition of fruitful intellectual work than the knowledge of anatomy is the precondition for correct walking (1949:115). About a decade later, Cooley expressed Weber's sentiments more pointedly when he wrote that

methodology is a little like religion. It is something we need every day, something we are irresistibly impelled to talk and think about, but regarding which we never seem to reach a definite conclusion. Each one, if he

> is clever, works out something adequate for his own use, but the more general principles remain unsettled. . . . Others help us far more by their example than by their theory. It would appear that a working methodology is a *residue* from actual research, a *tradition* of laboratories and work in the field: the men who contributed to it did so unconsciously, by trying to find something they ardently wanted to know. (1930:326. Italics in original)

Among more recent sociologists, Sorokin has long criticized "the 'slavish imitation' of physical science by psychosocial scholars" who

> seem to forget . . . that none of the established natural sciences has reached its maturity by merely imitating another science, especially when it is quite different. Each of them has built itself—in its basic concepts, uniformities, methods, and techniques—by following its own path corresponding to the nature of the phenomena studied. (1956:175)

He was joined in this view by Gurvitch and Timasheff (Timasheff, 1967:290). Dennis Wrong reflects Sorokin's "go it alone" and Cooley's informality arguments by asserting that past outstanding sociological theorists

> did not deliberately set out to create a science of sociology patterned on the physical sciences . . . [but] succeeded in creating a new discipline . . . in a fit of absentmindedness. (1963:316–17)

Arnold Rose has more recently repeated the Cooley argument as follows:

It is generally believed among scientists that, while theory varies with the investigator and is mutable, method is universal and immutable. . . . [perhaps because] within any one of the established physical or biological sciences, one method or combination of methods has proved to be the most appropriate to the subject matter, and even centuries of changes in theory and in the advancement of knowledge have not shaken the supremacy of this method. (1967:207–8)

Herbert Blumer, though inclined to a single (subjective) method, writes that the so-called scientific method of the physical and biological sciences is actually an area of difference, ambiguity, confusion, and controversy. In the social sciences and psychology, method variously comes to mean logical procedures (as in logic of sciences texts), general procedures (such as quantification or laboratory experimentation), or special procedures (such as operationalism or input-output models) (1966b: iv).

Following a position long held by Blumer and others that each method contains its own theoretical perspective, Norman Denzin rejects Merton's implication that method is neutral (Denzin, 1970:4) and argues for the "logic of triangulation" (1970:26–27, chap. 12): that many methods be used simultaneously in studying social phenomena (1970:12–14). The basis for triangulation is that the investigator, in selecting a particular research "method" (e.g., survey, participant observation, laboratory experiment), will "make different kinds of observations, engage in different analyses, ask different questions, and—as a result—may reach different conclusions" (1970:12). Underlying this proposition is the argument that any given method is not confined to just one set of causal influences

—it is not "free of rival causal factors"; thus, methods equipped to reveal the "different aspects of empirical reality" must be used, for Denzin sees this as compatible with the use of the "multiple operationalism" proposed by Webb, Campbell, Schwartz, and Sechrest (1966:174, in Denzin, 1970:26–27).

Derek Phillips (1973) rejects any idea of a correct method for sociology or a correct way to be a sociologist. Because he considers the search for objective truth, causes, and patterns to be a natural science importation into sociology, Phillips examines current methods and techniques that assume causes and patterns and finds these to be highly invalid (1973:chaps. 1–4). Social life is seen to have a "form of life" of its own embodied in the common-sense language of human experience (1973: chap. 8); therefore, Phillips' "language" for sociology requires human reasons and purposes (1973:126) rather than impersonal causes and patterns. Hence, he argues for "abandoning method" (1973:chap. 9) by using *anarchism* (Feyerabend, 1970), a "knowledge without foundations" (Feyerabend, 1962), a pragmatic procedure not guided or bound by rules. Involved in this procedure are the use of play in its nonserious and expressive aspects, of poetry, and the use of argument as a means of social construction consistent with the logic of discovery.[4]

4. Phillips' rejection of the search for causes and patterns and of rules of procedure puts him at odds with others who share his concern for discovery. Thus, although influenced by phenomenologists such as Husserl and Schutz and sympathetic with the concern for discovery by ethnomethodologists such as Garfinkel and symbolic interactionists such as Blumer, Phillips disagrees with the goal of Garfinkel and Blumer for discovering patterns and regularities and with their emphasis on rules of procedure (Phillips, 1973:138, 145–46). Much credit is given by Phillips to other ethnomethodologists such as Alan Blum (1970), Peter McHugh (1968, 1970), Thomas Wilson (1970a, 1970b), and Blum and McHugh (1971).

The existence of a scientific method has been frequently questioned in similar ways by philosophers and scientists. Norman Campbell, a British physicist and philosopher of science, stated over a half century ago that should a scientific study arrive at truth but violate logical formulas for method, the latter rather than the former is deficient (1952:47). C. Wright Mills (1959:58) wrote that the philosopher William Beck and the physicist Polykarp Kusch fail to locate a single method. D. W. Peetz argues that the methodologies of the various sciences bear only a "family resemblance" to one another, that we ought not be bewitched by "The Scientific Method" (quoted in Dixon, 1973:18). Edo Pivčević, a Yugoslavian philosopher living in Britain, sees sociology sharing minimal rules of scientific procedure with all sciences but asserts that this "unity of science" cannot be based on the absolute supremacy of natural, particularly physical, science as the paradigm for all others to follow (1972:335–37). Abraham Kaplan, an American philosopher of science, agrees, writing that the British mathematician and statistician Ronald A. Fisher noted in 1953 that a particularly successful *technique* in one or another field of science will come to dominate scientific method (1964:28); Kaplan warns against what he calls "the law of the instrument," i.e., give a small boy a hammer and he will find that everything needs pounding. Even Percy Bridgman, a physicist, operationalist, and one of logical positivism's "models," had written that "the scientist has no other method than doing his damnedest" (Kaplan, 1964:27).

A good summary of the issues, and one relevant to Kaplan's distinction between "reconstructed logic" and "logic-in-use" (see pages 114 and 125 in this chapter), is made by Scriven:

This is the logician's perennial temptation—make the portrait neat and perhaps the sitter will become neat. Usually there is more to be learnt from a study of disarray than is gained by intentionally disregarding it. The point is the same for logicians or for astronomers who wished to stuff the planets into circular orbits—judgments of neatness are very much more subjective than judgments of accuracy. . . . (1961:93n)[5]

Some Issues

One factor contributing to the dispute is the differential response to diversity in phenomena and to the methodological difficulties to which this leads. Single method advocates, with a "unified science" assumption and ideal, tend to assume such difficulties are surmountable with time and hard and ingenious work. Sometimes taking a *nominalist* or *fictionalist* view, they see arguments about the diversity of subject matter as either impractical or as the height of metaphysics (e.g., Lundberg, Catton). In contrast, multiple method advocates, often assuming a *realist* position, argue for the differences in subject matter between disciplines such as "natural" versus "cultural" sciences (e.g., Dilthey, Cooley, Sorokin, Blumer), or, on a more practical level, even within a given discipline (e.g., Feynman, Scriven).

A second basis for contention is the relevance of the distinction between *method* and *technique*. Defining scientific method abstractly enables single method advocates to tolerate *diversity* in technique (as among electron bombardment, tissue staining, computer simula-

5. Similarly and more recently, Thomas R. Blackburn offers *sensuous intuition*—needed to understand wholistic, complex, multidimensional, "messy" phenomena—as a necessary complement to the *logical* (or intellectual) *abstraction* method that has dominated science (1971).

tion, and case study). Multiple method advocates, on the other hand, might see many or all of these techniques as *separate* methods.

A third issue, perhaps the most difficult to resolve, is the "extra-logical" basis behind the acceptance or rejection of the scientific method ideal. Both believers in science as the only road to "cognitive" knowledge (and, therefore, to progress) and adherents of "humanistic," "verstehen," "existential," or "phenomenologist" approaches are loyal to their ideal. Each side tends to be impervious to reasoning, logic, even to experience—given the emotive and/or value bases for its loyalty.[6]

A fourth issue is that of *formal* versus *pragmatic* criteria. Both single method and multiple method advocates posit a norm or an ideal as a "model" or "form" to be followed. Yet it is probably stultifying to do so. Most scientists behave more practically than idealistically as they adjust to the problem, the data, and the research conditions. As Deutscher writes, even scientific problems begin with an "itch" and then follow their own logic (1973:Preface, chap. 1). Kaplan distinguishes between "reconstructed logic" (what scientists, after the fact, say they do or ought to do) and "logic-in-use" (what they actually do) (1964:2–11). Paul Diesing, a philosopher and political scientist, advocates a descriptive approach to science, his advocacy of this leading to reactions of surprise, shock, and dismay by scientists, and to the accusation that he has no standards (1971:319). Practically speaking, the Cooley-Rose argument seems persuasive: a technique becomes successful, then popular, then

6. Perhaps it was the strong reaction to subjectivist methodologies (e.g., humanistic, verstehen) that led conventional scientists to lump many dissimilar systematic "objective" procedures of observation and measurement under the single label, "scientific method."

sacred. With the tendency to idealization, it then receives much lip service by many who clearly violate it and by others who use it imperfectly.

CONCLUSIONS

Advocacy of a deductive form for all theory (discussed in the first part of this chapter) is a norm that needlessly restricts intellectual or scientific activity. As with the question of single or multiple method(s), it is better to rely on pragmatic criteria and thus to leave the question of single or multiple form(s) of theory open for the foreseeable future.[7] The argument here, then, is not that a deductive structure or model for theory is incorrect, is always ill-fitting, and/or is to be discarded. Nor does it assume that the deductive structure or model has actually been used widely in practice, even in the natural sciences. Instead, it inveighs against what it believes to be a widely, and often covertly, assumed view that deductive theory is the ideal for all to follow and that many actually do so. Therefore, reexamination of the deductive model for theory is frequently needed since the occasional past warnings and criticisms by natural and social scientists, and by philosophers, of sole reliance on deduction have apparently left that ideal unshaken.

The difficulties of advocating a single scientific method (the subject of the second part of this chapter)

7. One of the negative consequences of multiple methods, theory, forms, and substantive theories is that this very variety makes some additional scientific goals less likely. Among these are developing better theoretical continuity, even within specific subject areas (cf. Merton, 1968:8–27 and chaps. 7 and 11) and devising better criteria, perhaps through use of formal standards, for cumulative development of knowledge (cf. Freese, 1972). A third traditional scientific goal, a high level of prediction, may be similarly affected.

are twofold. One is the problem of adhering to an *abstract* ideal, whether in science, in scholarship in general, or with any cultural phenomenon—apart from the value of that ideal. A second problem is a conflict between two or more different abstract ideals, whether their bases be philosophic, moral, esthetic. Hopefully, problems such as these can be resolved by pragmatic criteria, if only temporarily and provisionally for each person, social circumstance, or time period. Among these criteria might be the type of substantive problem, nature and variety of the data, problems of observation and measurement, constraints of the research situation, span of generalization of the findings, formalization requirements, or applicability to practical issues. Pragmatic criteria offer the best hope of finding at least a workable agreement among the Hempels and the Scrivens, the Kaplans, Lundbergs, and MacIvers, the Mertons and the Roses.

Idealization and formalization, even fetishism, appear to be inevitable in science and in scholarship, as in social life. The history of social movements and of culture generally indicates this. Yet, challenge to a dominant form—in science and in culture—is insufficient protection since a new dominant form may then come to replace the old. Therefore, continuing openness to alternate ideas and forms—in theory and in method—is required. Eternal vigilance is as necessary to scholarship as it is to freedom.

Actually, the burden should be placed on those who advocate one, or even two, pure ideals—scientific, humanistic, deductive, or other. *They* are the idealists, the formalists, the purists, the reifiers (cf. Marković, 1972). Let *them* defend their position rather than force others to deny their (the formalists') exclusive claim to legitimacy. The pure form advocates should advocate less and accomplish more.

PART **|||** *Ethical and Political Issues in Theory, Method, and Social Involvement*

Radical and humanist sociologist[1] attacks on "establishment" sociology, rising to a crescendo by the latter part of the 1960s (cf. Mills, 1959; Stein and Vidich, 1963; Smith, 1964; Horton, 1966; Sjoberg, 1967; Gray,

---

1. These include the Sociology Liberation Movement (SLM), the Union of Radical Sociologists (URS), New University Conference sociologists (NUC), "the Movement," and New Left sociologists generally. They espouse a sociology variously called "radical" (Horton, 1969b; Szymanski, 1970b; Deutsch, 1970), "humanist" (Harrell, 1967; Glass and Staude, 1972; Lee, 1973), "reflexive" (Gouldner, 1970: chap. 13; Dawe, 1973), and "critical" (Birnbaum, 1971; Jay, 1973; Anderson, 1974).

129

1968; Nicolaus, 1969; Friedrichs, 1970; Gouldner, 1970; Roach, 1970; Deutsch and Howard, 1970; Colfax and Roach, 1971; Goodwin, 1973), led to renewed soul-searching by many sociologists about the field's professionalism and moral responsibility. It also suggested questions about possible alternatives to the current Establishment. More recently, counterattacks by (mostly) liberal sociologists (cf. Robbins, 1969; Bardis, 1970; Bendix, 1970; Horton and Bouma, 1970–71; Sewell, 1971; Nettler, 1972; Hollander, 1973; Wrong, 1974) have helped broaden the discussion of the issues and raised other issues as well—including those of the danger of "overkill" by the liberal counterattack and of the "ideal" relation among radical, liberal, and conservative sociologists.

These attacks and counterattacks continue, suggesting the relevance of political and ethical dimensions in sociological theory. Some support may be given the political thesis by examining the political implications of some of the big (general) theories (see chapter 2 in this volume), the consensus-conflict controversy (chapter 3), and the left-wing predilections of the new humanists (chapter 4). Examination of other sociological approaches and advocates fails to support this, however. For example, political assumptions do not seem very relevant to empiricists and small theory practitioners (chapter 1). Neither are political distinctions apparent between single and multiple theory advocates (chapter 5) nor between advocates and opponents of a single theory structure or a single method for sociology (chapter 6). Further, while left-wing politics appears more characteristic of new humanists than of neo-positivists (chapter 4), the latter includes sufficient left-of-center inclinations so as to blunt or dilute a humanist versus positivist political distinction.

Yet, while sociological positions and advocacies do not necessarily imply political positions and advocacies, the radical-liberal controversy is real whatever its source; and it is worth examining, not the least for its theoretical and methodological import. In this section, chapter 7 analyzes the main radical criticisms of current sociology and the recent liberal (and some conservative) counter-criticisms of radical sociologists. Chapter 8 examines some of the issues involved in sociology's professionalism, public posture, and moral responsibility—e.g., interventionism, activism, ethical neutrality, ideology, abstentionism, and similar issues argued at least since Comte. Also, arguments are made for at least a tripartite sociology: for radical, conservative, and liberal sociologies as at least temporarily important for a viable sociology.

Before going on to chapter 7, some definitions of radical, liberal, and conservative sociology are needed.

A *radical* sociology is an openly ideological sociology, more so than are liberal and conservative ones. Contemporary industrial society is seen as inhuman and requiring major structural changes through political means, violent and revolutionary if necessary. The only test of sociological knowledge is in action—its usefulness in effecting needed changes. Assumed are the relativity and historical specificity of knowledge, values, human institutions, and personality. There is a confidence about the role of activism and mass participation in bringing about a humane, equalitarian society. Implied also is an abundance philosophy toward human and material resources.

A *liberal* sociology sees society as periodically reformable through the application of scientific knowledge gathered with the use of a pragmatic methodology. It is a secular outlook (in contrast to the outlooks of both radical and conservative sociologies) that emphasizes a free marketplace of competing ideas, facts, and theories. Also, it differs from the other two sociologies in that it separates societal or personal goals or values from professional means or norms such as free inquiry, objectivity, truth, breadth of outlook, and tolerance of diverse viewpoints. Thus, liberal sociologists have a more piecemeal, less all-encompassing or totalist outlook toward knowledge, values, and society.

A *conservative* sociology emphasizes the importance and presupposition of social order and cultural continuity. Conservative sociologists stress the role of community and tradition and the ubiquity and positive function of social inequality. A scarcity outlook toward human and material resources is posited. Conservatives are less optimistic about progress, particularly because of its unanticipated consequences. They are likely to have a low opinion of the current state of social knowledge and a sober, prudent attitude toward the application of knowledge, regardless of its validity.

7
Radical Attack and Liberal (and Conservative) Counterattack

THE RADICAL SOCIOLOGISTS' CRITIQUE

The target of attack by radical and new humanist sociologists is what earlier was called the "social problems" or "social pathology" approach (Mills, 1943) and what came to be seen as the liberal Establishment in sociology, as the "sunshine boys" (Smith, 1964). The rationale for sociology's existence and growth as an empirical and applied science in America was seen by the Establishment to be the application of scientific knowledge for the amelioration of presumed consequences of industrialization, urbanization, and immigration—e.g., disorganization, crime, suicide, divorce, corruption, anomie. "Social problems" became a frequently taught sociology course at the college level (cf. Podell, Vogelfanger, and Rogers, 1959).

First, and basic to radical sociologist attacks on the (liberal) Establishment, is the "static" view of society proffered by the Establishment. Establishment sociology views social phenomena as to be systems in balance which tend to restore that balance when "disturbed," rather than as basically units of interaction, process, conflict, and change (Deutsch, 1970:86; Goodwin, 1973:7). Consistent with this is the idea of the individual as passive receptor and reactor to outside factors (A. Biblarz, 1969:2), as in many behavioristic, attitude, survey, small group, and organizations research. Nor is this a neutral conceptualization of society; the Establishment has come to *value* its static view, therefore to treat it as a *goal* (Gouldner, 1970:421–25). In other words, the concept of society as system or order has become a value for preserving order, in the tradition of Comte and Durkheim. Establishment sociology therefore is engaged in *reification* and *mystification,* in ideological justification of capitalist society (Horton, 1969a; Szymanski, 1970a:3, 8).

Related to the above is a further criticism, that all deviations from the static (and ruling) model of society will be treated as problematic, if not pathological. Thus Establishment sociologists tend to blame (and study) the "victim" rather than society or the ruling class for social problems. The "problem" becomes not society but the victim, the deviant, the minority, or the oppressed person who is unable to "make it" within society or to realize society's values (Horton, 1966, 1969a:11; Deutsch,

1970:86). This is often admitted by Establishment types
(e.g., Sibley, 1971:15). In this manner, American race
relations becomes the Negro problem, not the white problem (Bennett, 1965). "Riot control" research and "counterinsurgency" research of domestic and foreign "deviants" is carried on by U.S.-supported social science
(*Insurgent Sociologist,* 1969:2, 1970:5; Colfax, 1970:8;
Brown, Kahn, and Schulman, 1971:1; Johnson, 1971:3).
In Russia, dissidents are hospitalized as mentally ill.
Prestigious theoretical support is given the "deviant as
problem" view by Talcott Parsons, who considered the
checking of tendencies to deviance to be a requisite of
social systems (1951:28–30). (Szymanski sees an approach such as that of Parsons to be "totally useless as a
source of practical knowledge. . . . [It] finds its uses
solely as a legitimizing mechanism for the dominant interest structure [1970a:4; cf. Szymanski, 1972:148–50]).
A more extreme presumption in favor of conformity was
held by George Lundberg, for whom adjustment was the
normal state of all things, including science and society
(1939:5). Even Ross, Cooley, Mead, and the "Chicago
school," while more process-oriented, still tended to view
"disorganization" as requiring intelligent solution. Therefore, radical sociologists would preclude research on the
"oppressed" unless the latter agree with the purpose, approach, and follow-up action of that research (*Insurgent
Sociologist,* 1971:2).

   Another basis for attack on liberal Establishment
sociology is its technological approach to social problems
(Gouldner, 1968:114) and insufficient sensitivity to conflicting ethics or norms (Vaughan, 1967). Taking societal
goals for granted, sociologists have become professionals
(Gray, 1968:184; McKee, 1970–71:9–10), social en-
gineers who support the current value system in supplying

society with scientific tools. They have come to sell their service to the "haves" in studying the "have-nots" (Szymanski, 1970b:5–6; Dornbusch, 1970–71:113–14). Even the more radical are tempted and sometimes coopted (Horton, 1969a:11; Schevitz, 1970). Seeing themselves as disinterested scientists (Jacobs and Brown, 1970:6; Andreas, 1971:5; Etzkowitz, 1971:5; Porter, 1971:6) and frequently quoting Weber on objectivity and ethical neutrality (Hoult, 1968:6), Establishment sociologists are actually arrayed against drastic reform— certainly against revolution—and see society as perfectable or modifiable only through gradual change (Deutsch, 1970:85). As more social scientists began to be called on by industry and government, their role was largely one of supplying useful techniques to their clients (see Lazarsfeld, Sewell, and Wilensky [1967:Introduction] for an example of the "client" outlook) so as to manage social problems (Nicolaus, 1969:155; Colfax, 1970–71:76; McKee, 1970–71:9). Daniel Bell (1960) exemplified the tendency to see the modern age as beyond ideological disagreement and as properly concerned only with developing more efficient techniques. Thus, terms like "capitalism," "imperialism," and "exploitation" are treated by the Establishment as biased and ideologically intrusive; this is not the case with Establishment favorites like "productivity," "authority," and "counterinsurgency" (A. Biblarz, 1969:4; Horton, 1969a:9; Schevitz, 1971: 306). The combination of concern with order (or orderly progress) and the technological approach can be seen in the U.S. State Department's naming of foreign revolutions and coups as "trouble spots."

Related to the foregoing is the claim that sociological researchers have been careless and callous about their obligation to, and the feelings of, the subjects whom they study (Gouldner, 1968; Brown, 1969; Nicolaus, 1969: 155). Sometimes, subjects are not told they are being studied, research is misrepresented to them, or promises are broken (Erikson, 1967; O'Neill, 1970:103; Friedrichs, 1972:452). The investigator, more interested to "climb the university totem pole" and "to appear as the high priest of American society" (Deloria, in O'Donnell, 1971:1), thus gains the confidence of respondents by stressing the benefits of the research to them (or to their community) and by promising both anonymity and later disclosure of the general findings. Often, all three understandings are violated in the interest of the investigator and/or his financial or institutional backers (e.g., Vidich and Bensman, 1964:327–28; Horowitz, 1967b; Sjoberg, 1967:passim). In all this, an Establishment elitism is implied in that sociologists see themselves as detached Olympians standing above naive subjects—the latter not able to think or act sociologically (Fasola-Bologna, 1970: 39–40). There is disparaging of experiences "as they appear to those who live in them" (Ducey, 1970:3) whereas "oppressed groups . . . usually understand their experience better than the sociologists do" (Jacobs and Brown, 1970:6). In any case, recent signs give evidence of increased resistance, passive and violent, to playing "guinea pig" (Etzkowitz, 1970:120; O'Donnell, 1971:4).

A criticism from a broader historical perspective condemns the piecemeal and fragmented view of society by some sociologists and "social pathologists," their low-level theoretical abstraction making for nonstructural, atomized, social psychological approaches to social issues (Lynd, 1939:chap. 2; Mills, 1943:166–71, passim, and 1959; Deutsch, 1970:90). Such a view can result from the individualist conception of society long dominant in American economic, political, and religious philosophies;

from a pragmatic conception of change which tends to nominalistic views of social life; from the greater academic standing of biological and psychological disciplines; and/or from the fact that social structure is less "phenomenally real" to most people than are individual acts and interpersonal behavior. It also is conditioned by the reward system of bureaucratized-professional sociology that encourages the insignificant bits of research, the narrow perspective (Mills, 1959:chap. 5; Szymanski, 1970a:8; Becker and Horowitz, 1972:63). This criticism, a Marxist and neo-Marxist one, takes much current sociology to task for being nonstructural and nonhistorical and for having no overall theory of society other than a misguided functionalism (Mills, 1959:chap. 2). Related to this fragmented view of society is *disciplinary* fragmentation, the sociologists' narrow specialization keeping them ignorant of areas such as economics, history, and political science, without which it is impossible to make an overall analysis of modern society (URLA Newsletter, in *Insurgent Sociologist,* 1971:2; Andreas, 1971:4; I. Zeitlin, 1972:vi).

Finally, the liberal Establishment's commitment to science, even in its more moderate, less positivistic sense, is rejected by its critics.[1] In preferring the "humanist" to the "natural science" model of behavior, the new humanists reject much of current sociology's technology and formalization, both in theory (as in deductive theory and theory construction) and in methodology (such as mathematical sociology and the vast use of computers) (e.g.,

1. Cf. Mills, 1959; Stein and Vidich, 1963; Horowitz, 1964; Sjoberg, 1967; Gouldner, 1970; Etzkowitz, 1970; Goodwin, 1973:4; Willhelm, 1973:15; Willems, 1973:65. One exception is Szymanski who sees the "hard sciences" as the goal for sociology (1973:26), provided the historical specificity of social laws is recognized (*ibid.,* 30).

Cicourel, 1964; Bruyn, 1966; Sjoberg and Nett, 1968; Denzin, 1970). In all this, radical sociologists reject the Establishment's narrowness as to how research should be conceived, conducted, and presented. While humanistic sociology—in this more limited theory-method sense—has wide support among critics of the liberal Establishment, many of its practitioners do not share the Marxist outlook of the radical sociologists.

Thus, the liberal Establishment with its bureaucratized ways has lost sight of the human animal. This strain of criticism, common to both New Left and to more individualistic sociologists, argues against organizations and for small group—or even commune and underground church—settings wherein greater satisfaction, release, identification, and/or self-fulfillment can be obtained (Young, 1972:chap. 6). Man (and woman) the concrete rather than the abstract is the goal, sociology being challenged to become more authentic by making itself relevant to the "human condition" (cf. Mills, 1959; Stein and Vidich, 1963; Horowitz, 1964; Friedrichs, 1970; Andreas, 1971:5; Etzkowitz, 1971:5; Goodwin, 1973: 47). This, a form of individualistic "humanitarianism," opposes not only functionalist and behaviorist liberal Establishment types but also frequently structuralist and conflict Marxism and neo-Marxism. As already indicated (see chapter 4 in this volume), Bill Harrell, criticizing the positing of society's welfare and objective science as the ultimate goals, poignantly wrote

> In the last analysis, who gives a hang whether an institution is functional for society or not if it is not functional for all the men involved. Man is a social animal not for society's sake but for the animal's sake. (1967:120, note 20)

Implicit in many of the above criticisms is the historical argument of the rebel that, whatever its original basis for power, the Establishment no longer has authority to rule. Whatever the good intentions of the liberals in the past (e.g., Demerath, 1970:96), and putting aside for the moment their ideological weaknesses, the liberals are currently seen as having established entangling alliances with exploitative economic, political, and military interests (A. Biblarz, 1969:4; Colfax, 1970; Sperber, 1970:7); as "managing" new sociological movements by cooptation; and as studying quaint and manageable underdogs (cf. Gouldner, 1968, 1970; Nicolaus, 1969; *Insurgent Sociologist,* 1969:2; Jacobs and Brown, 1970: 6; Colfax, 1970–71). By stressing a static sociology and a static society, the liberal Establishment has impoverished the state of knowledge in the field and made it less relevant, even dangerous, to modern mankind. The Establishment's highly formalized and value-free science with its "fetishism" for objective concepts separated from human actions (Horton, 1969a), actually a disguised market ideology with a "sociology for sale" mien (Horowitz, 1963; O'Neill, 1972:171), has facilitated corporate capitalism's domestic neglect and international adventurism (cf. Nicolaus, 1969; Roach, 1970). Unless and until sociology changes theoretically and methodologically and returns to authentic social and human issues such as power and exploitation, it will have no authoritative basis for existence.

THE LIBERAL (AND CONSERVATIVE) SOCIOLOGISTS' RESPONSE

Most sociologists probably are neither radical nor conservative but range sociopolitically from moderate liberal to left liberal (cf. Glenn and Weiner, 1969:298–300; Lipset and Ladd, 1972:68–70; Orlans, 1973:2–6). While sharing some views with conservatives (e.g., continuity of society, emphasis on rules and order, some scarcity of resources), the sociological majority finds a greater degree of agreement with many radical assumptions and goals (e.g., progress, environmentalism, anti-racism, anti-business, educational reform, and a claim to know what's best for the "masses"). The areas of agreement between radical and liberal sociologists have made liberals more likely to back left-wing causes rather than conservative and right-wing ones. Historically, liberal sociologists were more inclined to support the civil liberties of union organizers, conscientious objectors, communists, socialists, and deviants from community manners and morals than the civil liberties of businessmen, army generals, farmers, and traditionalists of all kinds. Thus, while deviants across the political spectrum could legitimately be supported on the grounds of such basic liberal principles as freedom, individualism, and wider diffusion of power, a leftward bias was evident in the choice of deviants actually supported.

However, as the radical movement grew in the 1960s, both nationally and within sociology, liberals (even left liberals) found themselves less and less able to support radical programs and methods. As radicals grew in numbers, they no longer needed to compromise radical principles in order to obtain liberal support on a common popular front. In the early years of that decade, a wide popular front between radicals and liberals was still evident in the intensification of the civil rights movement in the early 1960s and, to some degree, in the growing opposition to Vietnam in the late 1960s. Even the more violent move toward greater student power found sociology faculties among the more willing to grant student demands. Further, substantial liberal support was given to sit-ins, demonstrations, and to the early stages of the black militancy movement, despite the violent nature of many of these activities. Nevertheless, as radical demands such as open admissions and abolition of grades and radical tactics such as villification and violence became sufficiently "illiberal," liberals (and liberal sociologists) began to withdraw from and to criticize the radical (and radical sociology) movement.[2]

One criticism by liberal (not necessarily Establishment) sociologists is that the "just" or humane society called for by radicals and humanists remains vaguely defined (Bensman, 1972:x; Hollander, 1973:148–49). Except for the communitarians, the new radicals have presented a much clearer picture of what they are against than of what they favor in a society (Manheim, 1973: 193). Presumably, the social characteristics of that society will be opposite to those of modern society. By implication, the new society will no longer have many characteristics of an industrial society such as mass production and distribution, large bureaucracies, and huge urban complexes. It will not feature impersonal, objective, macro bases for social order nor have externally or objectively based order at all. It will supposedly maximize possibilities for personal freedom and opportunity, enhance personal experience, and allow for fluid social

2. The liberal sociologist counterattack against radical socioologists was part of a more general liberal reaction against radical students, black militants, the New Left, and the counterculture that became evident in the years following the 1968 U.S. Presidential election. It has not abated as yet in the 1970s. Included in the counterattack were articles in liberal and left-liberal publications (e.g., *Commentary, New Republic, New York Times Magazine,* but not the *New York Review of Books,* the *New Yorker,* or *New York Magazine*) by sociologists such as Nathan Glazer, Andrew Greeley, Seymour Lipset, and Dennis Wrong.

relationships which are entered voluntarily (Young, 1972). At the same time, it would retain an upper-middle class level of living.

Nor do the new radical sociologists spell out believable paths to the new society (Spinrad, 1972:17). Some radicals assert or imply that voluntarism, egoism, and self-indulgence can bring about the new, just, and humane society. Others, having somewhat more of a blueprint for that society, feel that the important thing is to seize control of the power centers of society first, and to pass laws and initiate action programs second (cf. MacRae, 1971:6). (Thus, intent was important and, hopefully, a coherent plan as well.) Yet others, focusing more on their hatred for the present society (or "empire," cf. *Insurgent Sociologist,* 1969:3), emphasize disruption, sabotage, and destruction. The "cure" may be worse than the "disease" (a conservative argument used by liberals). Many sociologists, otherwise in sympathy with many radical goals, part company because of the above.

Next, the radical sociologists' call for relevance, their continual insistence upon moralizing, and their conscious ideological stance are attacked for question-begging, for narrowness, and for intolerance. The call for "relevance" begs the questions: "Relevant for what?" "to whom?" "in what circumstances?" (cf. MacRae, 1971:6). Are not typical sociological studies of crime, race, family, work, urbanism, and the like relevant? As with many other terms—"pragmatic," "functional," "moral," "beautiful," —relevant is a relational term, the contexts for it changing frequently. Further, moral commitment cannot be confined to radical goals (Robbins, 1969:115; Demerath, 1970:99) such as equality, freedom, human fulfillment, and exposure of corporate power, of exploitation, or of imperialism (Ehrlich, 1970; Szymanski, 1970c:21).

Moral commitment can also be made to conservative, right-wing, aristocratic, traditionalist, and/or nihilist goals such as profits, monopoly, elitism, infanticide, the patriarchal (or matriarchal) family, racism, fascism, or genocide. To exclude any goals but their own, radical sociologists would need to institute a totalitarian regime (Robbins, 1969:157; Horton and Bouma, 1970–71:32–33) that would exclude all ideologies except those espousing or implying equality, freedom, and fulfillment. Open ideology politicizes a field, tends to fragment social science positions into countless political factions (Orlans, 1973:13; Wrong, 1974:30), and leads to attempts to create ideological uniformity (Gove, 1970:222; Horton and Bouma, 1970–71:32–34; Hollander, 1973:150). Wrong-thinking and/or -acting sociologists would be rejected or rehabilitated by the fraternity—whether the errors referred to politics, to manners and morals, or to sociological knowledge and method (*Insurgent Sociologist,* 1969:4).

Related to the above is the impatience shown by radical sociologists and students (cf. Sewell, 1971:112) in calling for "instant action," as if moral and ideological fervor alone will suffice (Catton, 1972:444; Wrong, 1974:29–30). The constant call for structural change as a solution for every social evil, a "surgery for each hangnail" attitude, often becomes a copout, an excuse for doing nothing but criticize, pass resolutions, and demonstrate. In effect, social structure and cultural context are ignored and/or seen to be evil (Spinrad, 1972:4). True, many radical sociologists call for revolution while working with the poor, the black, and the ethnic in the local community (e.g., Colfax, 1970–71) but this cannot often be said of many younger radicals (Robbins, 1969:158; Willems, 1973:68). This impatience also manifests itself in the predilection for "instant, intuitive sympathy and understanding"—what Shils calls the "sacredness of immediate experience" (Bendix, 1970:832)—glorifying ignorance and know-nothing attitudes at the expense of diligent inquiry and work. Perhaps because of a reaction to pedantic education, "bourgeois" knowledge, and much of the formalism and tedium of modern life, short shrift is given by many radicals to any idea or plan of action that is not easily grasped, that does not immediately "turn one on" (S. Biblarz, 1969:14; Catton, 1971:85–86)— a subjectivist and self-indulgent attitude (Bernstein, 1972:86). Reflecting some of mass society's worst aspects—hedonism, consumerism, and immediate gratification (Catton, 1971:86)—the impatience and "presentism" makes many new radicals unreliable for organized and sustained action.[3]

An associated criticism is that radical sociologist programs exhibit vast ignorance of sociology and related disciplines (Bardis, 1970; Winthrop, 1971:261– 62), for example: the role of social continuity from the past (P. Berger, 1971:3; Wrong, 1974:27); the relative slowness (and interrelatedness) of most change; social, personal, and physical prerequisites for social life (cf. Catton, 1972). Radical sociologists assume that knowledge sufficient to bring about the "just" society exists, that intent to do so should then follow; therefore, all sociologists should drop what they are doing and join the radical unity of theory, method, and praxis (Demerath, 1970:95; Winthrop, 1971:26; Sibley, 1971:17). Radical sociologists, especially the younger ones, thus appear to have an "abundance" view of humans, society, and the

3. Richard Robbins refers to radical lack of historical lessons and perspective as an outlook that "everything began yesterday and will end tomorrow" (1969:157).

nonhuman environment—i.e., that the latter have practically inexhaustible resources and possibilities (Zurcher, 1970–71:61; Catton, 1971; Frankel, 1973:930)—and think that progress can be made on all fronts without losses, incompatibilities, or correlated evils (Hollander, 1973:152) (recent radical concern with pollution and "ecology," a "scarcity" and "incompatibility" approach to resources, might well be generalized by new radicals to society, economics, and political activism).

Another criticism, one characteristically made by liberals, is that radical sociologists violate their own (and the liberals') professed values: (1) undemocratic procedures are used in radical meetings and organizations; (2) the most blatant distortions are made in their publications, newsletters, and press releases; (3) much secrecy, stealth, and subterfuge exist in the treatment of nonradicals (Becker and Horowitz, 1972:54); (4) in the name of humanity and "the people," abuse is heaped upon those who disagree, often tending to dehumanize them. Essentially, the radical sociologists are very concerned with attaining personal advancement and power. Thus, radical sociologists vie with everyone else for grants, publications, tenure, promotion, and salary (Dotson, 1971: 262). Radical students and sociologists escalate their demands as soon as earlier demands are met. Further, when their disruption and violence are resisted by the authorities, the radicals yell "repression" (*Insurgent Sociologist,* 1969:8; Bendix, 1970:838).[4] In general, radi-

4. In the U.S. political scene of the 1970s, for example, all efforts by cities and universities to defend against violent demonstrations and bombings are given as evidence of increasing repression. This, the view that the victim of a righteous attack should take it lying down (Tyrmand, 1970:143), may be seen in the September 1970 Palestinian guerrilla airplane hijackings. Because of defensive precautions taken by Israel, El Al was the only airline whose planes resisted successfully a hijack attempt, thus leading to Palestinian guerrilla protests over armed guards on El Al's planes.

cals see American society as increasingly repressive when, in the view of liberals, there has never been as much freedom—in sexual behavior, in dress, in education, and in political activity. Seldom have Stouffer's and Merton's "relative deprivation" and Durkheim's "overexcited anomic" been more clearly illustrated. The repression argument has long been raised by activists, sometimes to enlist sympathy and support. Finally, arousing the authorities to repressive measures has long been a left-wing method, based on the assumption that a wave of right-wing repression must intervene between capitalism and socialism.

Last is the criticism that radicals have abandoned intellectual discipline and science altogether (Lidz, 1970: 14–15, 1972:51–52; Demerath, 1970:97–98) and have embraced irrational philosophies (Frankel, 1973) as did conservatives earlier in the history of science and social science (cf. Bandyopadhyay, 1971:23; Toby, 1971: 307–08). This is a likely pitfall in the social sciences (Lidz, 1970:13). Objectivity goes by the board (Bandyopadhyay, 1971:12–13, 24) as any kind of systematic methodology is distrusted and precluded (Demerath, 1970:98), treating all knowledge as if it were nothing but a perspective or construction of reality (Nettler, 1972:3; Frankel, 1973:929) and thus avoiding the long, hard, and disciplined work and expectations of only slow progress characteristic of science (Catton, 1971:86–87). Many assertions and charges are made without supporting evidence (Becker and Horowitz, 1972:65). Whatever the accusations, their truth is assumed to be evident and/or part of everyone's experience (cf. Robbins, 1969: 157; Horton and Bouma, 1970–71; 26–28). Many ideas about human nature, ruling classes, and exploitation are taken as true without indication that these pre-conceptions have been or will be examined or tested (Lidz, 1970:14). Often, criticisms by radical sociologists go beyond institutions and focus on the motives, bad values, and bad faith of capitalists, administrators, and most other sociologists. Much labeling and name-calling occurs (cf. *Insurgent Sociologist,* 1969:4); the guilt of the criticized is often seen as self-evident from their statuses, dress, hair, body attitudes, or speech.

SOME HISTORICAL BACKGROUND

To a great degree, the liberal-radical differences inhere in differing generational experiences (Sewell, 1971: 111–12): cultural, sociopolitical, and sociological. Culturally and sociopolitically, most American liberal sociologists experienced the depression of the 1930s, or at least World War II; they also remember vividly the threats, struggles, and compromises of the subsequent Truman and Eisenhower periods. As "older" or "middle-aged" liberal sociologists (and parents), they lean toward many of the following: the desirability of material progress, meritocracy, equal opportunity, free expression and dissemination of ideas, human relations and ethnic integration, applied knowledge, beneficent federal government, and cold war and collective security assumptions. On the other hand, most American radical sociologists experienced only the later years of the Eisenhower decade and emphasize the compromises and defensive stratagems employed by their liberal and Old Left professors and parents. Taking the gains of the previous decades for granted, assuming society's resources to be practically unlimited, and seeing anticommunism as a "sham," the new radicals moved in the 1960s from active civil rights struggles to more violent antiwar activities and eventually to revolutionary commitment. In contrast to their elders, the new radical sociologists oppose materialism, bourgeois manners and morals, organization, and science; they see American society as imperialist, racist, and repressive —as not worth saving.

The older generation feels that it has been through a period of youthful idealism and agitation before. It sees the younger generation as historically ignorant and, in any case, as unsociological in assuming that it (the younger generation) would have acted differently in the problems and circumstances of the earlier decades. The younger generation's conviction that it would have acted differently is implicitly a biological or bio-psychological argument since to have acted "better" than the older generation under the same circumstances implies innate superiority on the part of the young. The radical sociologists, in turn, see the older generation as having compromised and sold out its own principles (Keniston, 1968:309); and more importantly, as intellectually, morally, and emotionally ill equipped to deal with present and future exigencies.

The different sociologies of liberals and new radicals further increase the gulf between them. In order to support new radical sociologists' activism fully, most (liberal) sociologists, whether old or young, would need to forget what they consider valid and relevant sociological knowledge and its associated ethics. Thus, liberal sociologists would have to ignore what they believe to be true about social life (and what new radicals call bourgeois sociology): the multiplicity and intricacy of causes and effects, the historical continuity of social life, the social and personal requirements (external order as well as freedom) for societies, the relative slowness of change, and the likelihood of unexpected (and often unwanted) consequences of planned—particularly revolutionary— change. They would need to adopt a complete "abundance" view of nature, society, and human behavior.

Moreover, liberal sociologists would have to give up, or at least to compromise, professional and personal ethics and norms such as intellectual curiosity, free inquiry, truth, accuracy, breadth of outlook, universalism, and tolerance. These ethics and norms have been seen by the new radicals as, at best, middle-class and affluent luxuries (amenable to the radical charge that liberals are open to the *discussing* of a variety of alternatives but not to the *acting* upon them) and, at worst, as counterrevolutionary. To liberals, the radicals' lack of concern with the above ethics suggests a commonality between radicals and the more right-wing members of the "power elite"—for example, power-orientation, tendencies toward oligarchy, centralized control of all ideas and of political activity, and crass propaganda (cf. Marcuse, 1966:chap. 1 and passim).

Liberal sociologists have thought of themselves as a professional, anti-business, socially conscious elite; and not as pro-business, capitalist, or even Establishment. Accustomed to being in control of the discipline and profession, they have not shirked from giving condescending prescriptions to business and labor, to deviants and minorities, and to the huddled masses yearning to breathe free. They also have been accustomed to being praised and rewarded for their efforts, more recently by the business, political, and military sources that gave liberal sociologists succor, prestige, and a little power—and that encouraged tendencies toward glamorizing business and government through bureaucracy studies, organizational analysis, operations research, information theory, and systems analysis.

The initial response of many liberals to the radical charges and criticism, as already indicated, was to support many radical demands. Eventually, the incompatibilities described above created a dilemma for the liberal sociologists, causing many to pull back. Finally, liberals began to criticize radicals, first in terms of liberal principles (e.g., free inquiry, meritocracy, tolerance), then in terms of conservative principles as well (e.g., continuity of society, functional necessity of rules, limited possibilities and resources). It is possible that the increasing gulf between new radical sociologists and (old and new) liberal sociologists will lead the latter not only to reemphasize liberal principles more forcefully, but also increasingly to use more conservative ones—though the presence and size of radical sociologists has shielded liberals from conservative attacks. The near future may well see liberal sociologists, for defensive reasons at least, increasingly receptive to conservative and right-wing politics and sociology (e.g., Spencer, Sumner, Giddings, Lundberg, Van den Haag, Nisbet, Catton, Eckland). To the new radical sociologists, such a development would reveal the liberals' true colors to one and all; however, it might actually be more a case of a radical self-fulfilling prophecy.

CONCLUSIONS

Both radical attacks and liberal (and conservative) responses and counterattacks have revived or intensified the ethical and political issues in sociological theory and method. The following chapter discusses some of these issues, including their historical background; it offers a moderate—perhaps fatalistic—solution to these "perennial" issues and argues for at least a tripartite (radical, liberal, and conservative) sociology as inevitable and even useful for the field.

8 *Ethics and Politics: Perennial Issues, Possibilities, and Dangers*

THE EARLIER INTERVENTIONIST-ABSTENTIONIST DEBATE

The radical-liberal controversy discussed in the previous chapter broadens the issues of the earlier liberal-conservative debate in sociology "won" by the liberals. That debate was over the feasibility of using sociological knowledge to reform social life. The liberal or *interventionist* position, expounded by Ward and Cooley (and described in the previous chapter), was a progressive one that emphasized social melioration and human plasticity. The interventionists implied an *abundance* model of human and material resources. While value-free with respect to the conduct of science, this did not apply to the application of scientific findings to social melioration. As citizens or applied scientists, therefore, interventionists manifested greater activism and optimism toward guided social change.

The conservative or *abstentionist* position, stated most forcefully by Spencer and Sumner, stressed geographic, biological, and economic limitations and constraints upon social life. Culture, institutions, and social organization were seen as conserving and restraining forces. The abstentionists, assuming a *scarcity* model of physical and human resources, saw severe limitations on human possibilities and hence upon social and political reform. A value-free or ethically neutral stance was taken not only toward the conduct of science but toward social melioration as well. As scientists, sociologists were to abstain from social intervention. As citizens, while freer to suggest application of scientific findings, they were to do so carefully and soberly, mindful of the limited positive effects of human intervention.

The debate between interventionists and abstentionists (or liberals and conservatives) that had dominated sociology, however, was of less moment in practice; thus, the interventionist or liberal victory was less pure. Differences between interventionists and abstentionists became a matter of degree of, and conditions for, intervention. Interventionists, given to ameliorating problems through government, foundation, and university programs, often had their conception of the plasticity of the individual and society tempered by sociological knowledge and the intractability of society. Abstentionists, although still suspicious of social experiments and "do-goodism" and still emphasizing hard limits (e.g., biological and demographic factors, geographic and ecological factors, and economic variables) on active reform (cf. Hauser and Duncan, 1959; Hauser, 1960; Duncan and others, 1960; Duncan, 1964; Eckland, 1967a, 1967b) have apparently abandoned the Spencer-Sumner laissez faire philosophy while adopting a more restricted and less sanguine interventionism (cf. Lundberg, 1947:10–13, 109–12; 1964: 24–35; Van den Haag, 1963; Nisbet, 1966, 1968; Catton, 1971:83–85, 1972). Today, the difference between interventionists and abstentionists is one of degree, between a moderate *abundance* view and a moderate *scarcity* view toward human and material potential, respectively.

To liberal (i.e., moderate interventionist) sociologists, the issues raised by current radical sociologists about values, activism, and ethical neutrality are therefore old ones, sufficiently argued and settled in the past. Liberals resent being called conservative by radicals, given the activist assumptions behind their interventionist victory over the abstentionists (conservatives). To radical sociologists, on the other hand, the interventionist-abstentionist controversy was naive and narrow, if not immoral, in its treatment of ethical and political issues. It was naive in confining the issues to intervention versus abstention, to reform versus neutrality. It was narrow in taking for granted the current society as the setting for sociological activity. Finally, it was immoral in neglecting human suffering. This immorality is further displayed in the compromises that liberals made in triumphing over the abstentionist ideas, i.e., the liberals incorporated many characteristics of the conservatives (abstentionists) to form a weak "synthesis."

MORE RECENT FORMULATIONS

Myrdal, Kaplan, and Israel: A Humane Establishment Position

A more sophisticated approach to values, activism, and ethical neutrality than the radical, liberal, and conservative debates is the position held by Gunnar Myrdal, Abraham Kaplan, and Joachim Israel. These writers extend the Weberian ideal of the fact-value distinction and reflect Weber's struggle with the application of that distinction in practice. They propose that values (i.e., subjectivism or bias) can be reduced only to a degree and that selection must be made among values. In the early 1940s (as well as more recently), Myrdal argued that values are unavoidable—many are even desirable—and that they permeate social research and inquiry. Thus, the obligation of the social scientist is to attempt to state (confess) his or her value premises explicitly and concretely (1944:1043, 1059–60; 1969:chaps. 11–13). For Myrdal, science is not a matter of passive discovery of preexisting facts and laws but an active construction. Part of this activity, which includes definition, classification, selection, and inference, should also be the ferreting out of values (1944:1057, 1969:9). This provides a rationale not only for the statement and direction of theoretical research but also for subsequent practical application, such as social and political engineering (1944: 1043–45, 1059–60).

Myrdal's position is stated more clearly in Kaplan's *The Conduct of Inquiry* (1964), a philosophy of science text from a pragmatic perspective that has been very influential in sociology. Kaplan more explicitly develops Myrdal's argument that one must face involvement of values in scientific inquiry rather than attempting to exclude them. The many roles of values in science should be noted and their actual role in the research process examined (1964:387). For Kaplan, value is involved not only in studying values as subject matter but also in selecting problems for inquiry, defining what a fact is, and selecting one kind of interpretation over another (1964:377–86). Nevertheless, care can be taken (1) to *characterize* the values that are studied rather than to *appraise* them (Nagel, 1961:492–93, in Kaplan, 1964: 378), (2) to prevent value premises from causing the prejudging of problem solutions, and (3) to recognize alternate interpretations—though one must readily grant that values are not thereby eradicated but remain and play some causal role.

Not all values imply *bias,* according to Kaplan, who distinguishes between the scientist's *motives* (which go beyond the process of scientific inquiry) and *purposes* (which do not). Bias refers only to motives that relate inquiry to "the whole stream of conduct of which it is a part," to "interests external to the context of inquiry itself"—such as love of country, of money, or of glory (1964:374). In contrast to motives, the scientist's purposes are more limited in that they refer to special values or interests. Hence, purposes relate inquiry "to the particular scientific problem which they are intended to solve," for example, to show that a given explanation "can be extended to a certain other class of cases" (1964: 374). Consistent with this view of value is Kaplan's further argument that some ethics or values inhere in scientific inquiry—e.g., truth, honesty, integrity, judiciousness, caution, and conscientiousness (1964:379–81).

Joachim Israel, a Scandinavian sociologist, makes a value-norm distinction that is compatible with Kaplan's motive-purpose distinction (Israel, 1972). Values, or value-sentences, refer to something that is "good" and thus often signify an end or condition that is wanted. Norms or norm-sentences, in contrast, refer to "oughts" and therefore include formal and material rules of scientific activity as well as of models, constructs, and operational definitions (1972:70–78). The use of values by Israel would appear akin to Kaplan's "motives" as extra-scientific bias and his use of "norms" akin to Kaplan's "purposes" as means or methods necessary to scientific activity. Both Kaplan's "purpose" and Israel's "norm" are compatible with scientific objectivity, whereas "motive" and "value" are not (Israel, 1972:70). John Kultgen makes a similar distinction between motives intrinsic and motives extrinsic to science (1970:182).[1]

Lynd, Mills, and Horowitz: A Modified Activism

A more activist role for the social scientist was held by Robert Lynd and, more recently, by C. Wright Mills and Irving L. Horowitz. Seeing contemporary problems as incapable of solution if left to private capital, Lynd called for extension of democracy to all institutions and industry and for a revitalization of society, culture, and human personality via democratic planning (1939:chap. 6). To accomplish this, the gap must be closed between the broad and leisurely paced scholar-scientist, on the one hand, and the narrow and hurried practical technician, on the other. Without deprecating the humanities or education, Lynd called for social science to hasten its efforts. Social scientists should respond to social and hu-

1. A recent survey of social scientists, where bias was seen as more likely in the realm of action or policy formation than in actual research (Orlans, 1973:6–7), lends some support to Kaplan's, Israel's, and Kultgen's distinctions.

man priorities rather than to university administrators and business interests that tend to define much free inquiry and research as radical and/or subversive (1939: chap. 1).

C. Wright Mills wrote that "democracy implies that those vitally affected by any decision men make have an effective voice in that decision" (1959:188) and called for social scientists to turn their "explicit attention to a range of public issues and of personal troubles," to seek causal connections between milieux and social structure (1959:129–30). A clear and total exposure should be made of which (and whose) values are being imperiled, by whom, and of the degree of awareness of this by the various parties involved. Once the problem has been laid out and the relevant issues developed, then one can examine "the 'levers' by which the structure may be maintained or changed" and assess "those who are in a position to intervene but are not doing so" (1959:130–31).

Those in power, according to Mills, must therefore be impressed with their responsibility for the consequences of their actions. The general public must be shown the connection between its personal troubles, on the one hand, and public issues and structural trends, on the other (1959:184–88). The ideal role for the social scientist is that of an independent rather than a philosopher-king or an adviser to kings. Philosopher-kings emphasize reason but are too aristocratic. Advisers to kings emphasize rationality at the expense of moral and intellectual integrity. In contrast to these two roles, the role of the independent implies doing one's own work, choosing one's own problems, and directing this work *at* kings as well as to publics (1959:179–81). Therefore, a social scientist following the independent role is the most likely to use social science as a public intelligence apparatus to relate public issues to private troubles within contemporary structural trends (1959:181).

Irving Louis Horowitz, following Mills' large-range legacy, identified Mills and himself as reflecting the "occupationalist" or pragmatist (e.g., "Chicago school") wing of sociology, as opposed to the "professionalist" (e.g., "Columbia school") wing. The professionalist wing emphasizes a positivistic orientation; an elementaristic view toward data; bureaucratic team research; a view of sociology as a systematic, serious, and austere profession; and a value-free norm (1964:3–17, 1967a:361–63). In contrast, the occupationalist (pragmatist) wing leans toward sociology as a craft or discipline. As such, an occupationalist sociologist "has a more affective approach toward the object of his study, and his disposition is towards [sic] developing theories of behavior" (1967a: 361), not ignoring the heritage of the "classic tradition" (1964:18–19), yet desiring "connection, guidelines to action, and the kinds of outer directed experiences" that relate him to a directly concerned public (1967a:364). The occupationalist is geared toward action, feels a responsibility toward the public (but without a "sacred" air toward public institutions), is more critical of sociology and society, and is more free in methodology. Hence, occupationalists (and Horowitz, other Millsians, and sympathizers) feel themselves entitled to study anything of "relevance," to examine questions of value, to be more open methodologically, and to be less reluctant to cooperate with other disciplines (such as history, biography, and literature). Not only does this approach plunge the sociologist into human (including political) issues but it encourages different levels of insight and talent, thus enhancing the quality of sociological analysis as well (1964: 18–32, 1967a:372–74). Thus, Horowitz offers an intellectually differentiated and sophisticated modification of activism that rivals the humane modification of Establishment sociology and social science by Myrdal or Kaplan.

ETHICS AND POLITICS, AGAIN

Continual Disputes and Their Possible Outcomes

The disputes over ethics and politics have led to a variety of responses, as did controversies over theory and method (described in chapters 5 and 6). Radical and humanist sociologists are very confident in suggesting that definite solutions exist to questions of value, activism, abstention, and neutrality. Liberal sociologists offer a general value or goal (i.e., progress) and focus on abstract means or norms for achieving it (e.g., free inquiry, breadth of outlook, tolerance). Conservative sociologists, taking for granted the current social structure and long-established sociological practices and findings, have been less self-conscious about these issues.

One possible but unlikely outcome of ethical and political controversy in sociology is *resolution* of the issues, perhaps through the victory of one side or by integration of the competing sides. Sociology's past fails to afford much hope for resolution of controversy, however. Even the triumph of interventionist or liberal sociology over abstentionist or conservative sociology more than a half century ago was not decisive. Dissident and minority viewpoints (e.g., abstentionist and Marxist sociologies) have continued, and "settled" issues have recurred frequently.

A *dialectical* process of conflict resolution may be

a more apt interpretation of the history of controversies. From this view, ethical and political disputes in sociology (and theory and method disputes as well) have had periodic resolution, usually by some kind of integration or synthesis by the contending sides. Each resolution is said to be historically and socially specific in that it is a temporary solution of issues applicable only to its own time and social circumstances.[2] For example, the earlier interventionist-abstentionist controversy was solved by an interventionist triumph, though one that required some interventionist compromise with abstentionist principles (see pages 154–55 of this chapter). Similarly, the current controversy (with interventionist or liberal sociology as thesis and radical sociology as antithesis) would eventually achieve a resolution, presumably one that would be a modification or integration of both liberal and radical positions. As with the resolution interpretation, however, the dialectical one accounts only for the dominant perspective, not for dissident or minority perspectives that fail (or refuse) to integrate (e.g., conservative sociology).[3]

Although a dialectical interpretation adds insight to the history of ethical and political disputes, it should be supplemented by a *cyclical* one wherein the same con-

2. Each resolution is made in terms of what Mannheim (1936) called a perspective, epistemology, and/or ideology; what Kuhn (1962, 1970) has called a paradigm. Each successful perspective is influenced by "extra-theoretical" factors, i.e., it is the perspective of a particular age, class, or generation (Mannheim, 1936:268–79).

3. Since, in a dialectical interpretation, opposition (antithesis) comes from within the system, any minority perspectives external to that system are defined as survivals or relics that should at most be tolerated. People are thus expected to conform to the dominant perspective during its period of vitality, a position compatible not only with Hegel, Marx, and Mannheim but also with evolutionary theories that imply "survival of the fittest" such as those of Spencer and Sumner.

troversies are seen to arise in almost every generation. While resolution of some issues does occur,[4] it is often low level or trivial, temporarily supplying a basis for unity. Other issues, usually more abstract ones, have remained unresolved for thousands of years while the same, familiar arguments have been raised repeatedly. Among these issues are neutrality, objectivity, elementarism versus wholism, and nominalism versus realism.[5]

Possible Guides

To the degree that history shows both dialectical and cyclical processes, it offers little more than a general guide for the future. There will be no "end of ideology"; disputes will continue but one will not always be sure which issues are the more "concrete" ones subject to dialectical resolution and which are the more "abstract" ones that follow a cyclical pattern. It therefore becomes difficult for individuals to devise rules for coming to decisions about values or valuing—e.g., when to violate or follow a norm, when to invite arrest, when to be "true" to a position or to abandon it, when to betray a trust, when and how to involve and commit others, and when to remain neutral. Each era, social circle, and person needs to solve issues of values, involvement, ideology, and neu-

4. Among these are the interventionist "victory" mentioned earlier, the acceptance of quantitative methods by the end of World War II, and the recognition of theorizing and theory construction as legitimate activities by the early 1950s.
5. Neutrality has sometimes arisen as an area of compromise between opponents who agree to define that area as beyond dispute and to name certain functionaries to operate within it (e.g., arbitrators, judges, scientists, "strangers") (Wrong, 1974:30). Objectivity is often the position of the dominant or governing interest which is able to establish its own standard of objectivity; actually, it is a covert or disguised ideology as many such as Marx, Mannheim, and Sorokin have argued. The issues of elementarism versus wholism and nominalism versus realism have been discussed in parts 1 and 2 of this book.

trality for itself, in terms of its own situation. Undoubtedly, changing events and the exigencies of particular social settings and historical epochs will help to determine
the kind and proportion of people taking various positions
—conservative, liberal, radical, or other. Thus, valuing
and value issues continue to exist, to trouble, and to excite. Regardless of structural and historical arguments
and explanations for a given value position, no final rule
or set of conditions for value relevance and application
can be set up in anything but a very general sense: e.g.,
one should abandon neutrality (or any given interest or
ideology) when it "no longer applies."

Some Possibilities and Dangers

A more immediate issue—and a danger—is the
weakening of radical sociology by liberal overkill. It may
be time for liberal sociologists to "let up" on their counterattack lest they smother their radical colleagues. There
probably never was much likelihood that radical sociology would dominate the field. Indeed, recent signs indicate
a radical retreat from dialogue and radical despondence.
This may be judged by the decline of radical resolutions
at professional meetings, by the reduced activism on college campuses, and by the "demise of the Sociology Liberation Movement and the Union of Radical Sociologists," though not of the periodical *Insurgent Sociologist*
(cf. Porter, 1973:3). The radical movement is at least
beyond its utopian stage (cf. Friedrichs, 1972:454).
Noteworthy is the fact that the number of radical cau-
cuses and of radical and humanist sections at the American Sociological Association meetings has not declined
(see note 4 in chapter 4 of this volume).

From the standpoint of liberal sociologists, any re-
duction of radical influence in sociology might well be re-

placed by increased conservative influence. To the degree that such a shift would merely balance sociological viewpoints among radicals, liberals, and conservatives, it would benefit the field; conservative sociology has been weak in recent decades. Yet, should radical sociology be made impotent, with or without the aid of liberals, a new ideological struggle between liberals and conservatives might emerge.[6] Rather than receiving valuable ideas from its conservatives, sociology might then find itself involved in another heated and excessive ideological and political struggle, this time between liberals and conservatives.

The viewpoint of this book is that sociology benefits from a variety of perspectives, ideological and other; each perspective offers an outlook, and perhaps a method, not significantly duplicated by the others. Among current perspectives are the radical, liberal, and conservative. A radical sociology emphasizes the role of (naked) power and exploitation and the unity of theory in "praxis" in manipulating power and mass participation to bring about structural change and a humanistic society. A liberal sociology stresses orderly progress in a secular society by way of application of scientific knowledge gained through an open, pragmatic methodology. Finally, a conservative sociology emphasizes social order and continuity, human and environmental limits upon knowledge, and prudence in applying knowledge. (See the introduction to part 3 of this volume for a more extended definition of these three sociologies.)

6. The absence of a conservative sociology large enough for radicals to attack has exposed the liberal majority to radical attack and to radical labeling of liberals as really "conservative." Conversely, the absence of a viable radical sociology would expose liberals to conservative attack and to being labeled "radical" by conservatives. Therefore, a healthy liberal sociology would require significant radical and conservative wings.

What may be best for the field is a pluralistic sociology, at least a tripartite one. Further, if one of the three is to be a "first among equals," let it be liberal (rather than radical or conservative) sociology for the following reasons:

1. Liberal values for openness and steady progress are closest to those of (Western) science and, presumably, sociology (cf. Hoult, 1968:3, 4).

2. Liberalism's "central" location (i.e., between radicals and conservatives) is most likely to make for endurance of all three.

3. Liberal sociologists are the most likely to "tolerate" the other two.[7]

CONCLUSIONS

Establishments are vulnerable to attack and dissection. The more the Establishment is closed and totalitarian, the more will criticism of it be credible; universally held; covert and informal; and expressed with sadness,

---

7. A radical sociology tends to active intolerance of conservatives (defined broadly so as to include many liberals); it seeks to eliminate diversity in outlook, goals, and method. A conservative sociology, on the other hand, is intolerant in a more passive sense in that it ignores and excludes radicals (defined broadly so as to include many liberals)—as did the German University in the days of Marx and Weber; it would discourage innovation and disrespectful dissection of society. Whereas Establishment sociology is seen as primarily conservative and reactionary by radical sociologists (*Insurgent Sociologist,* 1969:3, 1970:3), its detached and secular (i.e., nonrespectful) study of sacred institutions and spheres of life (e.g., family, church, local community) has usually made it appear disturbing, even dangerous and radical, to conservatives and the general public (cf. Braude, 1970:234; Rossi, 1970–71:123; P. Berger, 1971:2–3). In any case, the results of sociological activity are likely to be seen as biased, and, therefore, differentially criticized by the variety of interests and viewpoints affected by its findings (A. Biblarz, 1969:4; Becker, 1971:13).

humor, and even detachment. In contrast, the more liberal, open, and beneficent the Establishment, the more controversial, esoteric, open, and heated the criticism; and the more likely is the criticism to come from the deviant, the rebel, the alienated, and/or the elite (cf. Tyrmand, 1970:chaps. 6, 7).[8] The sociology Establishment, a relatively open and tolerant one, has been attacked repeatedly by a relatively powerful and affluent minority. The attacks revived consideration of age-old issues such as activism, neutrality, and ideology—and the feasibility of alternatives to Establishment sociology. Inevitably, there was a reaction to the attacks, largely from liberal (Establishment and other) sociologists.

The issues raised are old ones that have not been and probably cannot be given a universally applicable solution. Hence, there exists the revived, perennial debate between sociological generations. Moreover, liberal sociologists are advised to refrain from succeeding "too well" in attacking their radical colleagues; a viable well-rounded sociology needs not only a liberal perspective, but a radical (and conservative) one as well.

In conclusion, ethical and political issues have always been involved in sociological theory and method. Sometimes these have been discussed openly and heatedly, as in the contemporary situation. Often the issues

---

8. When establishments emphasize values such as neutrality and objectivity, they become especially vulnerable to attack. This is because the neutrality and objectivity imply colorless norms such as detachment, minimal involvement, pure cognition, and fact-orientation. Adherents of such values and norms are easily put on the defensive by others committed to political or moral positions. Yet, neutrality and objectivity are necessary and useful to all sides, particularly during times of frequent, heated conflict. Even the most committed political or moral position requires an area of fact-orientation where cognition can be distinguished from evaluation (cf. Catton, 1971:81; Nettler, 1972:3).

have been dormant, their formulation and solution taken for granted. While definite political and ethical standpoints do not follow directly from most existing sociological positions in theory and method, ethical and political considerations are implied in sociological analysis and periodically need to be faced and reformulated.

9
Conclusion: Diversity, Polarity, Empiricism, and Small Theories

One of current sociology's main characteristics is the continual expansion of its theory. This expansion includes significant activity in large and small theories and in concepts and typological analysis. Moreover, the empiricism (i.e., inductive logic) of most actual research, as well as the diversity of theoretical activity, is obscured by the attention paid a few large (i.e., general) theories. Also, much controversy and polarity still take place, which leads to critical examination of the field not only from theory and method standpoints but from ethical,

169

political, and sociology of sociology perspectives as well (e.g., Friedrichs, 1970; Gouldner, 1970; Reynolds and Reynolds, 1970).

THEORETICAL ALTERNATIVES

Given the variety in the field, the theoretically concerned sociologist has several possible alternatives:

1. To apply one major theory or school to all of sociology, as is the case with structure-functionalists, Marxists, integral theorists (Sorokin), and pluralistic behaviorists.

2. To select a theory or school that is seen as dealing with the most relevant social phenomena and remain within its confines (e.g., symbolic interactionism and organizational, exchange, and ecological theories).

3. To be eclectic, using different theories, large and small, for different phenomena and/or circumstances.

4. To create new theories, constructing these to apply to data (e.g., Blalock, 1969; Berger, Zelditch, and Anderson, 1972; Gibbs, 1972b).

5. To engage in more modest activities such as typology, concepts, and the like (e.g., Loomis, McKinney, Nisbet, Rosenberg, Boskoff).

6. To use various inductive approaches to derive theory from facts or from empirical generalizations (Znaniecki, 1934:chap. 6; Glaser and Strauss, 1967). This alternative appears to be the most frequent one in current sociology.

The argument of this work is closest to alternative 3, the eclectic approach, for it contends that analysis of diverse theories can lead to a rational basis for using different theories for different problems or data (cf. Wallace, 1969:pt. I; Warshay, 1971b:204). Alternative 1, in stressing that a single theory be used for all social phenomena, is not feasible because no single theory has as yet been shown to fit the diversity of social life. Alternative 2 is appealing in that it does not claim the universe and, therefore, does not promise to handle all phenomena. Alternative 4, unfortunately, is likely to repeat the single theory emphasis of alternatives 1 and 2. Alternative 5 is useful, but a typology approach is too limited a theoretical attack. Alternative 6 is empiricist, thus having the advantage of open-mindedness; yet its very open-mindedness often means uncritical (because unexamined) use of categories, assumptions, epistemologies, and ideologies. Thus, the empiricist-inductivist, while open to the charge of automatically and unwittingly supporting the scholarly and political status quo, at the same time offers some hope for a pragmatic and careful development of theory out of research.

Sociology should attempt all the above alternatives. A multiple approach could be encouraged in books, journals, meetings and conventions, and graduate training. While the theoretical alternatives presented here are not mutually compatible, no single theorist need attempt them all. The increasing number of sociologists permits diversity, and the growing internationalization of sociology and the field's invasion of new "applied" and/or "content" areas make it inevitable.

CURRENT THEORETICAL TRENDS

Summary of Trends

Of the main trends referred to in this work, the more important ones appear to be:

1. the empiricist (inductive) nature of most sociology

2. the dominance of theoretically informed and guided research by small theories

3. the increased philosophical, and even ideological, polarization of the field

4. the persistence of latent micro theory despite some macro tendencies, much of micro theory relying on attitude and opinion variables

5. the decline of theories featuring value and norm in favor of those featuring interaction, organization, and exchange, with very recent emphases on behavioristic and reinforcement approaches and technologies

6. some increased interest in diverse areas such as theory construction, Marxist and neo-Marxist analyses, and social phenomenology

7. a shift of some interdisciplinary efforts from social psychology toward economics, politics, the noncultural environment, demography, and even biology, demonstrating greater ease in transcending disciplinary boundaries

8. a tendency toward *empirical* resolution, at least in principle, of some theoretical disputes, as may be seen in the work of Cole, Edel, Lenski, Lukes, Schrag, and Van den Berghe

9. continual integration attempts (e.g., micro theory with macro theory and consensus theories with conflict theories)

10. an increasingly common vocabulary which encourages typological analysis

11. the development of both rigorous (formalistic) and loose-jointed (humanistic and pragmatic) methodologies—the former featuring theory formalization, computer simulation, and mathematical sociology; the latter

featuring participant observation techniques, strategy of multiple methodologies, and phenomenological analysis

12. continuing challenges to the hierarchical (deductive) model for theory and to a single, identifiable scientific method (but not to the single, general, integral theory ideal)

13. little increase in the level of prediction, degree of theoretical continuity, and amount of cumulative knowledge

14. an increased opportunity for theory to cover more content areas and more societies

15. a heightened awareness of ethical and political dimensions in sociology

16. the tendency for most sociologists to be practical and detached from controversy, doing empiricist research or using small theories in their own limited areas of interest

Reactions

Reactions to the trends listed above are informative about the current state of theory. For example, there appears to be little objection to the tendency toward a common vocabulary (item 10), even though many continue to create new terms or redefine old ones. Nor does there seem to be disagreement with the view that theory should be more continuous and predictive and that sociological knowledge should be more cumulative (item 13). Further, general support exists for the view that sociological theory needs to cover more content areas and, in particular, become international (item 14). Moreover, there is no apparent opposition to the tendency to empirical resolution of some theoretical disputes (item 8), though some skepticism might be expected. Also, an overwhelming majority of sociologists appears to favor theory integration attempts and, in contrast to trends in other disciplines, to expect and hope for a single, general, integral theory (item 9). Judging from the history of ideas, however, this degree of agreement will not last long.

The field appears to be more divided in its view toward small theories (item 2). On the one hand, they are seen as stimulators of research and stepping stones or bridges between data and general theory by, for example, Merton, Wallace, or Boskoff. On the other hand, small theories have been deemed low level and perhaps methodologically crude and unimaginative by Parsons, Horowitz, and, earlier, Sorokin or Timasheff. A similar division occurs in the attitude toward micro (item 4) and social psychological (item 7) emphases. Some, like Homans, T. Mills, or Bales, clearly lean toward the micro level, with its social psychological, small group, and even organizational emphases. Others, like Parsons, Etzioni, M. Zeitlin, and, earlier, Sorokin and C. W. Mills, have leaned toward the macro level and cultural, historical, political, economic, and demographic variables. When macro analysis transcends national and civilizational boundaries, the prestige of macro theory increases despite its lower "scientific" standing. A division along another dimension can also be seen. At one side are theories featuring social relationships and organization (e.g., organizational, exchange, ecological, and general systems theories). At the other side are theories featuring value and norm (e.g., structure-functionalism from a more deterministic perspective and integral theory and social phenomenology from a less deterministic one) (item 5).

Equally divisive as these theoretical disputes are ethical and political disputes (item 15), increased philosophical polarization of the field (item 3), the existence of both rigorous and loose-jointed methodologies (item 11), and challenges to the hierarchical theory model and to a single scientific method (item 12). The issues involved in two of these controversies—ethical-political issues and philosophic polarization—are openly acknowledged and discussed. The disputants, whether radical versus Establishment sociologists (item 15) or new humanists versus neo-positivists (item 3), clearly grant one another's existence and influence, if not always the other's legitimacy. In the case of the other two controversies—the existence of two kinds of methodologies and challenges to the hierarchical theory model and to a single method—there is some denial as well. Thus, as described in chapters 4 and 6, there is mutual recognition of the other in that humanist and neo-positivist methodologists criticize one another (item 11); but there is also denial of the other by omission in that many texts and courses give the impression that sociology has only one method and that theory has only one structure (item 12).

Finally, it seems characteristic of theorists (and of other participants in arguments over theory, method, ethics, and politics) that they criticize and disparage empiricism or inductivism (item 1) and the more narrow, practical sociological pursuits (item 16). Empiricists are derided as pedestrian by theory constructionists and conceptual architects who are perennially making impressive beginnings. Yet, empiricism can be sophisticated (as in the work of Glaser and Strauss, Garfinkel, or H. S. Becker); in any case, it can be the groundwork for further inductive, theoretical activity (item 1), particularly when supplemented by typological analysis (item 10). There is similar disdain for the practical sociologist who is detached from momentous issues and is given to research that is either empiricist or that uses small theories rather than large (item 16). This type of sociologist, however, by pursuing manageable problems in more specialized subfields of sociology, promises to contribute more to theory development in the near future. If one dominant characteristic of modern sociological theory exists, it is this one—inductive theoretical activity in more limited, practical research.

CONCLUSIONS

Variety and Controversy

In contrast with the monolithic appearance presented by sociology in the 1950s and early 1960s, the present period shows its variety. This variety is found not only in current theory and method but in ethical and political issues as well. The field thus (albeit reluctantly) tolerates multiple theories, methodologies, and value, aesthetic, and political approaches (cf. Wrong, 1971:252). Yet, this variety obscures the more modest, undramatic activity of the field, such as the useful and (potentially) cumulative research in sociology's many subfields.

Some Needed Balance

While controversy has restored a balance to many areas where only one viewpoint had dominated, other areas still appear to be one-sided. For example, small theories need more recognition relative to large theories. Also, more macro research is required to supplement the excessive reliance upon micro, particularly attitude and opinion, research. Moreover, alternatives to a single general theory, to a single form for theories, and to a single method should receive more emphasis.

The diversity and controversy within sociology has made the realization of three other goals difficult or impossible. The first of these goals is that of theoretical continuity; there is little, even within single subject areas. The second difficult-to-realize goal is that of the level of prediction contributed by sociological research. The third goal is that of developing better criteria for the cumulative development of knowledge. The three goals are very short of realization, and the theory and method variety and controversy are barriers to such realization. On the other hand, would theoretical continuity, prediction level, and cumulative knowledge improve materially in the absence of variety and controversy?

Some Consequences of Diversity and Polarity

Theoretical diversity troubles many. They seek to overcome it through integration, espousal of a single theory, or abandoning theory altogether. The field does not, therefore, lack self-critics, many of whom tend to be alarmed and/or intolerant (e.g., P. Berger, Catton, Friedrichs, Gouldner, Homans, Horowitz, Lundberg, C. W. Mills, Nicolaus, Sorokin). One disturbing tendency is that the increasing number of critics includes many who seem to engage in no additional sociological activity other than teaching. John O'Neill writes that "sociology must achieve a critical sense which avoids opportunism of the sort that comes from living *off* sociology rather than *for* it" (1972:168). A second "disturbing" tendency is for theories to go in or out of style, to be replaced rather than refuted (Eberts and Witton, 1970:1094, note 25) because their "domain assumptions" (Gouldner, 1970) or "paradigm" (T. Kuhn, 1962, 1970) no longer fit (Mannheim, 1936), no longer excite sociologists' "imagination, value and feeling" (Dawe, 1973:50).

Yet, there is room—even a necessity—for many views, regardless of the costs. Current theory is broad enough (and intellectually developed enough) so that it can contain positivists as well as humanists, large systematizers and the more narrowly focused, pure and applied, cross-disciplinarians and loyalists, and "basic" question-askers and technological experts. Sociological theory remains multifaceted not only because of the structural variety of social life but also because of the nature of knowledge. A deplorable but inevitable condition to some, to others it is a source of interest and intrigue.

References

Aage, Hans
　　1972　"Some reasons for and effects of the use of attitude-variables in sociological theory." *Acta Sociologica* 15 (4):342–65.

Abell, Peter
　　1971　Model Building in Sociology. New York: Schocken Books.

Aberle, D. F., A. K. Cohen, A. K. Davis, M. J. Levy, and F. X. Sutton
　　1950　"The functional prerequisites of a society." *Ethics* 9 (January):100–111.

Abrahamsson, Bengt
 1970   "Homans and exchange: Hedonism revived."
        American Journal of Sociology 76 (September):
        273–85.

Ackerman, Charles, and Talcott Parsons
 1966   "The concept of 'social system' as a theoretical
        device." Pp. 24–40 in Gordon J. DiRenzo (ed.),
        Concepts, Theory, and Explanation in the Be-
        havioral Sciences. New York: Random House.

Adams, Bert N.
 1966   "Coercion and consensus theories: Some unre-
        solved issues." *American Journal of Sociology*
        71:714–17.

Alihan, Milla A.
 1938   Social Ecology: A Critical Analysis. New York:
        Columbia University Press.

Anderson, Charles H.
 1974   Toward a New Sociology. Revised ed.; Home-
        wood, Ill.: Dorsey Press.

Anderson, III, Robert G.
 1967   "On genetics and sociology (II)." *American
        Sociological Review* 32:997–99.

Andreas, Carol
 1971   "Reply to Bendix speech." *Insurgent Sociologist*
        1 (April):4–5.

Andreski, Stanislav
 1965   The Uses of Comparative Sociology. Berkeley:
        University of California Press.

Bain, Read
 1962   "The most important sociologists?" *American
        Sociological Review* 27 (October):746–48.

Baldwin, James M.
 1895   The Mental Development in the Child and the
        Race. New York: Macmillan.

Bandyopadhyay, Pradeep
    1971   "One sociology or many: Some issues in radical sociology." *Sociological Review* (Great Britain), new series, 19 (February):5–29.

Bardis, Panos D.
    1970   "Campus unrest: History, knowledge, politics in college." *Social Science* 45 (October):223–27.

Bartholomew, David J.
    1967   Stochastic Models for Social Processes. London and New York: Wiley.

Bartos, Otomar J.
    1967   Simple Models of Group Behavior. New York: Columbia University Press.

Bates, Frederick L.
    1956   "Position, role, and status: A reformulation of concepts." *Social Forces* 34 (May):313–21.

Beauchamp, Murray A.
    1970   Elements of Mathematical Sociology. New York: Random House.

Becker, Howard P., and Alvin W. Boskoff (eds.)
    1957   Modern Sociological Theory in Continuity and Change. New York: Dryden.

Becker, Howard S.
    1967   "Whose side are we on?" *Social Problems* 14 (Winter):239–47.
    1970   Sociological Work: Method and Substance. Chicago: Aldine.
    1971   "Reply to Riley's 'partisanship and objectivity.' " *American Sociologist* 6 (February):13.

Becker, Howard S., and Irving L. Horowitz
    1972   "Radical politics and sociological research: Observations on methodology and ideology." *American Journal of Sociology* 78 (July):48–66.

Bell, Daniel

1960   The End of Ideology: On the Exhaustion of Political Ideas in the Fifties. Glencoe, Ill.: Free Press.

Bendix, Reinhard

1964   Nation-Building and Citizenship: Studies of Our Changing Social Order. New York: Wiley.

1970   "Sociology and the distrust of reason." *American Sociological Review* 35 (October):831–43. (1970 presidential address, American Sociological Association)

Bennett, Jr., Lerone

1965   "The white problem in America." *Ebony* 20 (August):29–36.

Bensman, Joseph

1972   "Foreword." Pp. v–xiii in Bernard Rosenberg, The Province of Sociology: Freedom and Constraint. New York: Crowell.

Berelson, Bernard, and Gary A. Steiner

1964   Human Behavior: An Inventory of Scientific Findings. New York: Harcourt, Brace & World.

Berger, Brigitte

1971   Societies in Change: An Introduction to Comparative Sociology. New York: Basic Books.

Berger, Joseph, Bernard P. Cohen, J. Laurie Snell, and Morris Zelditch, Jr.

1962   Types of Formalization in Small-Group Research. Boston: Houghton-Mifflin.

Berger, Joseph, Morris Zelditch, Jr., and Bo Anderson (eds.)

1966   Sociological Theories in Progress. Volume I; Boston: Houghton-Mifflin.

1972   Sociological Theories in Progress. Volume II; Boston: Houghton-Mifflin.

Berger, Peter L.
1963 Invitation to Sociology: A Humanistic Perspective. Garden City, N.Y.: Anchor Books.
1971 "Sociology and freedom." *American Sociologist* 6 (February):1–5.

Berger, Peter L., and Thomas Luckmann
1966 The Social Construction of Reality: A Treatise in the Sociology of Knowledge. Garden City, N.Y.: Doubleday.

Bernard, Jessie
1950 "Where is the modern sociology of conflict?" *American Journal of Sociology* 56 (July):11–16.
1962 American Community Behavior. Revised ed.; New York: Holt, Rinehart & Winston.

Bernstein, Richard J.
1972 "Critique of Gouldner's *The Coming Crisis of Western Sociology.*" *Sociological Inquiry* 42 (Winter):65–72.

Bertalanffy, Ludwig von
1950 "An outline of General System Theory." *British Journal of the Philosophy of Science* 1:159–64.
1968 General System Theory: Foundations, Development, Applications. New York: George Braziller.
1972 "The history and status of General Systems Theory." *Academy of Management Journal* 15 (December):407–26.

Biblarz, Arturo
1969 "On the question of objectivity in sociology." *et al.* 2 (Fall):2–5.

Biblarz, Sandra
1969 "Radical and conservative reform in the university." *et al.* 2 (Fall):13–14.

Bierstedt, Robert
1960 "Sociology and humane learning." *American Sociological Review* 25 (February):3–9.

Birnbaum, Norman

1967   "Eastern Europe and the death of God." *Commentary* 44 (July):69–73.

1971   Toward a Critical Sociology. New York: Oxford University Press.

Black, Max (ed.)

1961   The Social Theories of Talcott Parsons: A Critical Examination. Englewood Cliffs, N.J.: Prentice-Hall.

Blackburn, Thomas R.

1971   "Sensuous-intellectual complementarity in science." *Science* 172 (June 4):1003–7.

Blain, Robert R.

1971   "On Homans' psychological reductionism." *Sociological Inquiry* 41 (Winter):3–19.

Blalock, Jr., Hubert B.

1969   Theory Construction: From Verbal to Mathematical Formulations. Englewood Cliffs, N.J.: Prentice-Hall.

1971   (ed.) Causal Models in the Social Sciences. Chicago: Aldine-Atherton.

Blau, Peter F.

1964   Exchange and Power in Social Life. New York: Wiley.

1968   "Interaction: IV. Social Exchange." Pp. 452–58 in David Sills (ed.), International Encyclopedia of the Social Sciences. Volume 7; New York: Crowell-Collier and Macmillan.

Blum, Alan F.

1970   "Theorizing." Chapter 13 in Jack D. Douglas (ed.), Understanding Everyday Life. Chicago: Aldine.

Blum, Alan F., and Peter McHugh

1971   "The social ascription of motives." *American Sociological Review* 36 (February):98–109.

Blumer, Herbert

1938 "Social psychology." Chapter 4 in Emerson P. Schmidt (ed.), Man and Society. New York: Prentice-Hall.

1956 "Sociological analysis and the 'variable.' " *American Sociological Review* 21 (December): 683–90.

1962 "Society as symbolic interaction." Pp. 179–92 in Arnold M. Rose (ed.), Human Behavior and Social Processes: An Interactionist Approach. Boston: Houghton-Mifflin.

1966a "Sociological implication of the thought of George Herbert Mead." *American Journal of Sociology* 71:535–44. See also "Reply," *American Journal of Sociology* 71:547–48.

1966b "Foreword." Pp. iii–vii in Severyn T. Bruyn, The Human Perspective in Sociology. Englewood Cliffs, N.J.: Prentice-Hall.

1969 Symbolic Interactionism: Perspective and Method. Englewood Cliffs, N.J.: Prentice-Hall.

1971 "Social problems as collective behavior." *Social Problems* 18:298–306.

Bogardus, Emory S.

1960 "Selected sociological concepts for beginning students in sociology." *Sociology and Social Research* 44 (January):200–208.

1973 "Twenty-five years of American sociology: 1947 to 1972." *Sociology and Social Research* 57 (January):145–52.

Boguslaw, Robert

1965 The New Utopians: A Study of System Design and Social Change. Englewood Cliffs, N.J.: Prentice-Hall.

Borgatta, Edgar F. (ed.)

1969 Sociological Methodology 1969. San Francisco: Jossey-Bass.

Borgatta, Edgar F., and George W. Bohrnstedt (eds.)
1970   Sociological Methodology 1970. San Francisco: Jossey-Bass.

Boskoff, Alvin
1972   The Mosaic of Sociological Theory. New York: Crowell.

Bosserman, Philip
1968   Dialectical Sociology: An Analysis of the Sociology of Georges Gurvitch. Boston: Porter Sargent.

Bottomore, Thomas B.
1956   Classes in Modern Society. New York: Pantheon Books.
1966   Elites and Society. Baltimore: Penguin (originally published in 1964).
1968   "Marxist sociology." Pp. 46–53 in David Sills (ed.), International Encyclopedia of the Social Sciences. Volume 10; New York: Crowell-Collier and Macmillan.
1971   Sociology: A Guide to Problems and Literature. Second ed.; London: Allen and Unwin.

Bottomore, Thomas B., and Maximilien Rubel (eds.)
1964   Karl Marx: Selected Writings in Sociology and Social Philosophy. New York: McGraw-Hill (originally published in 1956).

Boulding, Kenneth
1962   Conflict and Defense. New York: Harper.

Bowman, Claude C. (ed.)
1973   Humanistic Sociology: Readings. New York: Appleton-Century-Crofts.

Bradley, Gerald P. and Robert R. Reynolds, Jr.
1970   "Reply to T. N. Ferdinand." *American Sociologist* 5 (November):345–47.

Braude, Lee
  1970   "Louis Wirth and the locus of sociological commitment." *American Sociologist* 5 (August): 233–35.

Brodbeck, May (ed.)
  1968   Readings in the Philosophy of Science. New York: Macmillan.

Brown, Carol
  1969   "From the washroom." Letter; *American Sociologist* 4 (May):158.

Brown, Carol, Roger Kahn, and Jay Schulman
  1971   "Apologia: Power structure research at Russell Sage." *Insurgent Sociologist* 1 (April):1, 7.

Brown, Julia S., and Brian G. Gilmartin
  1969   "Sociology today: Lacunae, emphases, and surfeits." *American Sociologist* 4 (November): 283–91.

Brown, Robert
  1963   Explanation in Social Science. Chicago: Aldine.

Bruyn, Severyn T.
  1966   The Human Perspective in Sociology: The Methodology of Participant Observation. Englewood Cliffs, N.J.: Prentice-Hall.

Buckley, Walter
  1967   Sociology and Modern Systems Theory. Englewood Cliffs, N.J.: Prentice-Hall.
  1968   (ed.) Modern Systems Research for the Behavioral Sciences. Chicago: Aldine.

Burgess, Ernest W.
  1953   Page 599 in Past Presidents, "Presidential advice to younger sociologists" (compiled by Samuel A. Stouffer). *American Sociological Review* 18 (December):597–604.

Burgess, Robert L., and Don Bushell, Jr. (eds.)
  1969   Behavioral Sociology: The Experimental Analysis of Social Process. New York: Columbia University Press.

Cameron, William B.
  1963   Informal Sociology: A Casual Introduction to Sociological Thinking. New York: Random House.

Campbell, Norman
  1952   What Is Science? New York: Dover (originally published in 1921).

Cancian, Francesca M.
  1968   "Functional analysis: II. Varieties of functional analysis." Pp. 29–43 in David Sills (ed.), International Encyclopedia of the Social Sciences. Volume 6; New York: Crowell-Collier and Macmillan.

Caplow, Theodore
  1954   Principles of Organization. New York: Harcourt, Brace & World.
  1969   Two Against One: Coalitions in Triads. Englewood Cliffs, N.J.: Prentice-Hall.

Catton, Jr., William B.
  1964   "The development of sociological thought." Chapter 24 in Robert E. L. Faris (ed.), Handbook of Modern Sociology. Chicago: Rand McNally.
  1966   From Animistic to Naturalistic Sociology. New York: McGraw-Hill.
  1971   "Sociology in the 1970's." *Australian and New Zealand Journal of Sociology* 7 (October):80–91.
  1972   "Sociology in an age of fifth wheels." *Social Forces* 50 (June):436–46.

Chapin, F. Stuart
  1928   Cultural Change. New York: Century.

Chinoy, Eli
    1954   Sociological Perspective: Basic Concepts and Their Application. New York: Random House.
    1968   Sociological Perspective: Basic Concepts and Their Application. Second ed., revised and enlarged; New York: Random House.

Cicourel, Aaron V.
    1964   Method and Measurement in Sociology. New York: Free Press.

Clark, Terry N.
    1972   "Emile Durkheim and the French university." Pp. 152–86 in Anthony Oberschall (ed.), The Establishment of Empirical Sociology. New York: Harper & Row.

Cohen, Percy S.
    1968   Modern Social Theory. New York: Basic Books.

Cole, Robert
    1966   "Structure-function theory, the dialectic, and social change." *Sociological Quarterly* 7 (Winter):39–58.

Coleman, James S.
    1964   Introduction to Mathematical Sociology. New York: Free Press.

Colfax, J. David
    1970   "Knowledge for whom? Relevance and responsibility in sociological research." *Sociological Inquiry* 40 (Winter):73–83.
  1970–71 "Some notes on local level political activism." *Sociological Focus* 4 (Winter):69–81.

Colfax, J. David, and Jack L. Roach (eds.)
    1971   Radical Sociology. New York: Basic Books.

Collins, Randall
  1972–73 "Surveying the sociological journals." *Change* 4 (Winter):70–74.

Cooley, Charles H.

1902   Human Nature and the Social Order. New York: Scribner's.

1930   Sociological Theory and Social Research: Being Selected Papers of Charles Horton Cooley. Robert C. Angell (ed.); New York: Holt.

Coser, Lewis A.

1956   The Functions of Social Conflict. Glencoe, Ill.: Free Press.

1963   (ed.) Sociology Through Literature: An Introductory Reader. Englewood Cliffs, N.J.: Prentice-Hall.

1967   Continuities in the Study of Social Conflict. New York: Free Press.

1969   "Unanticipated conservative consequences of liberal theorizing." *Social Problems* 16 (Winter): 263–72.

1971   Masters of Sociological Thought: Ideas in Historical and Social Context. New York: Harcourt Brace Jovanovich.

1972   (ed.) Sociology Through Literature: An Introductory Reader. Second ed.; Englewood Cliffs, N.J.: Prentice-Hall.

Coser, Lewis A., and Bernard Rosenberg (eds.)

1969   Sociological Theory: A Book of Readings. Third ed.: New York: Macmillan.

Costner, Herbert L.

1971   Sociological Methodology 1971. San Francisco: Jossey-Bass.

1972   Sociological Methodology 1972. San Francisco: Jossey-Bass.

1973   Sociological Methodology 1973. San Francisco: Jossey-Bass.

Costner, Herbert L., and Hubert M. Blalock Jr.

1972   "Scientific fundamentalism and scientific utility: A reply to Gibbs." *Social Science Quarterly* 52 (March):827–44.

Coult, Allan D., and Robert W. Habenstein
 1965   Cross Tabulation of Murdock's World Ethno-
        graphic Sample. Columbia, Mo.: University of
        Missouri Press.

Coulter, Jeff
 1971   "Decontextualized meanings: Current ap-
        proaches to *verstehende* investigations." *Socio-
        logical Review* (Britain), new series 19
        (August):301–23.

Coutou, Walter
 1949   Emergent Human Nature: A New Social Psy-
        chology. New York: Knopf.

Curtis, James E., and John W. Petras (eds.)
 1970   The Sociology of Knowledge: A Reader. New
        York: Praeger.

Cuzzort, Raymond P.
 1969   Humanity and Modern Sociological Thought.
        New York: Holt, Rinehart & Winston.

Dahrendorf, Ralf
 1959   Class and Class Conflict in Industrial Society.
        Stanford, Calif.: Stanford University Press.

Davis, J.
 1973   "Forms and norms: The economy of social rela-
        tions." *Man* (Great Britain) 8 (June):159–76.

Davis, Kingsley
 1959   "The myth of functional analysis in sociology
        and anthropology." *American Sociological Re-
        view* 24 (December):757–72. (1959 presi-
        dential address, American Sociological Associa-
        tion)

Dawe, Alan
 1973   "The role of experience in the construction of
        social theory; An essay in reflexive sociology."
        The Sociological Review (Britain), new series
        21 (February):25–55.

Demerath, III, Nicholas J.
    1970   "Sociology, science, and the passionate phoenix."
            Sociological Inquiry 40 (Winter):263–72.

Demerath, III, Nicholas J. and Richard A. Peterson (eds.)
    1967   System, Change and Conflict: A Reader on
            Contemporary Sociological Theory and the De-
            bate over Functionalism. New York: Free Press.

Denisoff, R. Serge, Orel Callahan, and Mark H. Levine (eds.)
    1974   Theories and Paradigms in Contemporary So-
            ciology. Itasca, Ill.: F. E. Peacock.

Denzin, Norman K.
    1969   "Symbolic interactionism and ethnomethodo-
            logy: A proposed synthesis." *American Socio-
            logical Review* 34 (December):922–34.
    1970   The Research Act: A Theoretical Introduction
            to Sociological Methods. Chicago: Aldine.

Deutsch, Morton, and Robert M. Krauss
    1965   Theories in Social Psychology. New York: Basic
            Books.

Deutsch, Steven E.
    1970   "The radical perspective in sociology." *Socio-
            logical Inquiry* 40 (Winter):85–93.

Deutsch, Steven E., and John Howard (eds.)
    1970   Where It's At: Radical Perspectives in Sociology.
            New York: Harper & Row.

Deutscher, Irwin
    1973   What We Say/What We Do: Sentiments and
            Acts. Glenview, Ill.: Scott, Foresman.

Diesing, Paul
    1971   Patterns of Discovery in the Social Sciences.
            Chicago: Aldine-Atherton.

Dixon, Keith
    1973   Sociological Theory: Pretence and Possibility.
            London: Routledge & Kegan Paul.

Dornbusch, Sanford M.

1970–71   "The coming failure of mission-oriented social research." *Sociological Focus* 4 (Winter):113–19.

Dotson, Floyd

1971   "Actions speak louder than words." Letter; *American Sociologist* 6 (August):262.

Douglas, Jack D. (ed.)

1970   Understanding Everyday Life. Chicago: Aldine.

Dreitzel, Hans P. (ed.)

1970   Recent Sociology No. 2: Patterns of Communicative Behavior. New York: Macmillan.

Dubin, Robert

1960   "Parsons' actor: Continuities in social theory." *American Sociological Review* 25 (August): 457–66.

1969   Theory Building. New York: Free Press.

Ducey, Mike

1970   "Insurgency versus sociology." *Insurgent Sociologist* I (August):3, 7.

Duncan, Hugh D.

1962   Communication and Social Order. New York: Bedminster Press.

Duncan, Otis D.

1964   "Social organization and the ecosystem." Chapter 2 in Robert E. L. Faris (ed.), Handbook of Modern Sociology. Chicago: Rand McNally.

Duncan, Otis D., and Leo F. Schnore

1959   "Cultural, behavioral, and ecological perspectives in the study of social organization." *American Journal of Sociology* 65 (September):132–46.

Duncan, Otis D., and others

1960   Metropolis and Region. Baltimore: Johns Hopkins Press.

Eberts, Paul R., and Ronald A. Witton

1970   "Recall from anecdote: Alexis de Tocqueville and the morphogenesis of America." *American Sociological Review* 35 (December):1081–97.

Eckland, Bruce K.

1967a   "Genetics and sociology: A reconsideration." *American Sociological Review* 32 (April):173–94.

1967b   "Reply to Beals and Anderson." *American Sociological Review* 32 (December):999–1001.

Edel, Abraham

1959   "The concept of levels in social theory." Pp. 173–94 in Llewellyn Gross (ed.), Symposium on Sociological Theory. Evanston: Row, Peterson.

Ehrlich, Howard J.

1970   "The 1969–1970 anti-ROTC offensive." *Insurgent Sociologist* 1 (August):4.

Eisenstadt, Shmuel N.

1965   Essays on Comparative Institutions. New York: Wiley.

Erikson, Kai T.

1967   "A comment on disguised observation in sociology." *Social Problems* 14 (Spring):366–73.

Etzioni, Amitai

1961a   A Comparative Analysis of Complex Organizations: On Power, Involvement and Their Correlates. New York: Free Press.

1961b   (ed.) Complex Organizations: A Sociological Reader. New York: Holt, Rinehart & Winston.

1969   (ed.) A Sociological Reader on Complex Organizations. Second ed.; New York: Holt, Rinehart & Winston.

1970   "Toward a macrosociology." Chapter 2 in John C. McKinney and Edward A. Tiryakian (eds.), Theoretical Sociology: Perspectives and Developments. New York: Appleton-Century-Crofts.

Etzkowitz, Henry

1970 "Institution formation sociology." *American Sociologist* 5 (May): 120–24.

1971 "Reply to Bendix speech." *Insurgent Sociologist* I (April):5.

Eubank, Earle E.

1932 The Concepts of Sociology. Boston: D. C. Heath.

Fairchild, Henry P. (ed.)

1944 Dictionary of Sociology. New York: Philosophical Library.

Fallding, Harold

1968 The Sociological Task: A Concise Introduction to the Main Issues in Sociological Theory and Method. Englewood Cliffs, N.J.: Prentice-Hall.

Fararo, Thomas J.

1973 Mathematical Sociology: An Introduction to Fundamentals. New York: Wiley-Interscience.

Fararo, Thomas J., and Morris H. Sunshine

1964 A Study of a Biased Friendship Net. Syracuse, N.Y.: Youth Development Center.

Faris, Robert E. L.

1961 "Reflections on the ability dimension in human society." *American Sociological Review* 26:833–43. (1961 presidential address, American Sociological Association)

1964 (ed.) Handbook of Modern Sociology. Chicago: Rand McNally.

1967 Chicago Sociology: 1920–1932. San Francisco: Chandler.

Fasola-Bologna, Alfredo

1970 "The sociological profession and revolution." *Sociological Inquiry* 40 (Winter):35–43.

Ferdinand, Theodore N.

1969 "On the impossibility of a complete general theory of behavior." *American Sociologist* 4 (November):330–32.

Feyerabend, P. K.
- 1962   Knowledge Without Foundations. Oberlin, O.: Oberlin Board of Trustees.
- 1970   "Against method: An anarchistic theory of knowledge." *Minnesota Studies in the Philosophy of Science* 4:17–130.

Feynman, Richard
- 1965   The Character of Physical Law. London: Cox and Wyman. Referred to on page 48 in Robert K. Merton, Social Theory and Social Structure. Enlarged, third ed.; Glencoe, Ill.: Free Press, 1968.

Filstead, William J. (ed.)
- 1970   Qualitative Methodology: Firsthand Involvement with the Social World. Chicago: Markham.

Firth, Raymond
- 1965   Primitive Polynesian Economy. Second ed.; London: Routledge and Sons.

Foote, Nelson N.
- 1951   "Identification as the basis for a theory of motivation." *American Sociological Review* 16 (February):14–21.

Frankel, Charles
- 1973   "The nature and sources of irrationalism." *Science* 180 (June 1):927–31.

Freese, Lee
- 1972   "Cumulative sociological knowledge." *American Sociological Review* 37 (August):472–82.

Friedrichs, Robert W.
- 1970   A Sociology of Sociology. New York: Free Press.
- 1972   "Dialectical sociology: An exemplar for the 1970s." *Social Forces* 50 (June):447–55.
- 1974   "The potential impact of B. F. Skinner upon American sociology." *American Sociologist* 9 (February):3–8.

Fromm, Erich
    1961   Marx's Concept of Man. New York: Frederick Ungar.

Galtung, Johan
    1964   "A structural theory of aggression." *Journal of Peace Research* (Oslo) 1 (2):95–115.
    1967   Theory and Methods of Social Research. Oslo: Universitetsforlaget.

Garfinkel, Harold
    1967   Studies in Ethnomethodology. Englewood Cliffs, N.J.: Prentice-Hall.

Garfinkel, Harold, and Harvey Sacks
    1970   "On formal structures of practical actions." Chapter 13 in John C. McKinney and Edward A. Tiryakian (eds.), Theoretical Sociology: Perspectives and Developments. New York: Appleton-Century-Crofts.

Geertz, Clifford
    1964   "The transition to humanity." Chapter 3 in Sol Tax (ed.), Horizons of Anthropology. Chicago: Aldine.

Gibbs, Jack P.
    1972a   "Causation and theory construction." *Social Science Quarterly* 52 (March):815–26.
    1972b   Sociological Theory Construction. Hinsdale, Ill.: Dryden Press.

Gittler, Joseph B. (ed.)
    1957   Review of Sociology: Analysis of a Decade. New York: Wiley.

Glaser, Barney G., and Anselm L. Strauss
    1967   The Discovery of Grounded Theory: Strategies for Qualitative Research. Chicago: Aldine.

Glass, John F., and John R. Staude (eds.)
    1972   Humanistic Society: Today's Challenge to Sociology. Pacific Palisades, Calif.: Goodyear.

Glenn, Norvall D., and David Weiner
    1969   "Some trends in the social origins of American sociologists." *American Sociologist* 4 (November):291–302.

Gluckman, Max
    1955   Custom and Conflict in Africa. Oxford: Blackwell Press.
    1965   Politics, Law and Ritual in Tribal Society. Chicago: Aldine.

Goldschmidt, Walter
    1966   Comparative Functionalism: An Essay in Anthropological Theory. Berkeley and Los Angeles: University of California Press.

Goldthorpe, John H., David Lockwood, Frank Bechhofer, and Jennifer Platt
    1969   The Affluent Worker in the Class Structure. London and New York: Cambridge University Press.

Goode, William J.
    1960   "A theory of role strain." *American Sociological Review* 25 (August):483–96.

Goodwin, Glenn A.
    1973   "The emergence of various theoretical trends and their prospects in sociology." *Sociological Focus* 6 (Spring):1–9.

Gorz, Andre
    1967   Strategy for Labor. Boston: Beacon Press.

Gould, Jay and William L. Kolb (eds.)
    1964   A Dictionary of the Social Sciences. New York: Free Press.

Gouldner, Alvin W.
    1955   "Metaphysical pathos and the theory of bureaucracy." *American Political Science Review* 49: 496–507.
    1959a   "Organizational analysis." Pp. 400–428 in

Robert K. Merton, Leonard Broom, and Leonard S. Cottrell, Jr. (eds.), Sociology Today: Problems and Prospects. New York: Basic Books.

1959b "Reciprocity and autonomy in functional theory." Pp. 241–70 in Llewellyn Gross (ed.), Symposium on Sociological Theory. Evanston: Row, Peterson.

1960 "The norm of reciprocity: A preliminary statement." *American Sociological Review* 25 (April):161–78.

1968 "The sociologist as partisan: Sociology and the welfare state." *American Sociologist* 3 (May): 103–16.

1970 The Coming Crisis of Western Sociology. New York: Basic Books.

Gove, Walter R.
1970 "Should the sociology profession take moral stands on political issues?" *American Sociologist* 5 (August):221–23.

Granovetter, Mark S.
1973 "The strength of weak ties." *American Journal of Sociology* 78 (May):1360–80.

Gray, David J.
1968 "Value-free sociology: A doctrine of hypocrisy and irresponsibility." *Sociological Quarterly* 9 (Spring):176–85.

Gray, Don
1972 "On the logical possibility of a quasi-general theory of behavior." *American Sociologist* 7 (May):6–7.

Gross, Llewellyn (ed.)
1959 Symposium on Sociological Theory. Evanston: Row, Peterson.

1967 Sociological Theory: Inquiries and Paradigms. New York: Harper & Row.

Gumplowicz, Ludwig
   1899   The Outlines of Sociology. Frederick W. Moore, translator; Philadelphia: American Academy of Political and Social Science.

Gurvitch, Georges
   1962   Dialectique et Sociologie. Paris: Flammarion.

Habermas, Jürgen
   1970   Toward a Rational Society: Student Protest, Science, and Politics. Jeremy J. Shapiro, translator; Boston: Beacon Press.
   1971   Knowledge and Human Interests. Jeremy J. Shapiro, translator; Boston: Beacon Press.
   1973   Theory and Practice. Translated by John Viertel. Boston: Beacon Press (originally published in Germany in 1971).

Hage, Jerald
   1972   Techniques and Problems of Theory Construction in Sociology. New York: Wiley.

Hare, A. Paul, Edgar F. Borgatta, and Robert F. Bales (eds.)
   1965   Small Groups: Studies in Social Interaction. Revised ed.; New York: Knopf.

Harrell, Bill
   1967   "Symbols, perception, and meaning." Pp. 104–27 in Gross (ed.), 1967, op. cit.

Hauser, Philip M.
   1960   Population Perspectives. New Brunswick, N.J.: Rutgers University Press.
   1969   "The chaotic society." *American Sociological Review* 34 (February):1–19. (1968 presidential address, American Sociological Association)

Hauser, Philip M., and Otis D. Duncan (eds.)
   1959   The Study of Population: An Inventory and Appraisal. Chicago: University of Chicago Press.

Hawley, Amos H.

1950　Human Ecology: A Theory of Community Structure. New York: Ronald Press.

1968　"Ecology: I. Human ecology." Pp. 328–37 in David Sills (ed.), International Encyclopedia of the Social Sciences. Volume 4; New York: Crowell-Collier and Macmillan.

1973　"Ecology and population." *Science* 179 (March 23):1196–1201.

Hempel, Carl G.

1959　"The logic of functional analysis." Pp. 271–307 in Gross (ed.), 1959, op. cit.

Hessler, Richard M., and Peter Kong-ming New

1972　"Research as a process of exchange." *American Sociologist* 7 (February):13–14.

Hinkle, Roscoe C., and Gisela J. Hinkle

1954　The Development of Modern Sociology: Its Nature and Growth in the United States. Garden City, N.Y.: Doubleday Short Studies in Sociology.

Hollander, Paul

1973　"Sociology, selective determinism, and the rise of expectations." *American Sociologist* 8 (November):147–53.

Holzner, Burkart

1968　Reality Construction in Society. Cambridge, Mass.: Schenkman.

1972　Reality Construction in Society. Revised ed.; Cambridge, Mass: Schenkman.

Homans, George C.

1950　The Human Group. New York: Harcourt, Brace & World.

1958　"Social behavior as exchange." *American Journal of Sociology* 62 (May):597–606.

1961   Social Behavior: Its Elementary Forms. New York: Harcourt, Brace & World.

1964a   "Bringing men back in." *American Sociological Review* 29 (Dec.):809–18.

1964b   "Contemporary theory in sociology." Chapter 25 in Faris (ed.), 1964, op. cit.

1967a   "Filling the hollow frontier." *et al.* 1 (Fall):2, 8.

1967b   The Nature of Social Science. New York: Harcourt, Brace & World.

1969   "Comment on Blau's paper." Pp. 80–85 in Robert Bierstedt (ed.), A Design for Sociology: Scope, Objectives, and Methods. Monograph 9; Philadelphia: The American Academy of Political and Social Science.

1971a   "Reply to Blain." *Sociological Inquiry* 41 (Winter):19–24.

1971b   "Rebuttal to Blain." *Sociological Inquiry* 41 (Winter):25.

Hopkins, Terence K.

1961   "Bureaucratic authority: The convergence of Weber and Barnard." Pp. 82–98 in Etzioni (ed.), 1961b, op. cit.

Horowitz, David

1969   Empire and Revolution: A Radical Interpretation of Contemporary History. First American ed.; New York: Random House.

Horowitz, Irving L.

1962   "Consensus, conflict, and cooperation." *Social Forces* 41 (Dec.):177–88.

1963   "Sociology for sale." *Studies on the Left* 3 (Winter):109–15.

1964   (ed.) The New Sociology: Essays in Social Science and Social Theory in Honor of C. Wright Mills. New York: Oxford University Press.

1967a   "Mainliners and marginals: The human shape of

sociological theory." Pp. 358–83 in Gross (ed.), 1967, op. cit.

1967b (ed.) The Rise and Fall of Project Camelot: Studies in the Relationship between Social Science and Practical Politics. Cambridge, Mass.: MIT Press.

1972 The Three Worlds of Development: The Theory and Practice of International Stratification. Second ed.; New York: Oxford University Press.

Horton, John

1966 "Order and conflict theories of social problems as competing ideologies." *American Journal of Sociology* 71 (May):701–13.

1969a "The fetishism of concepts." *et al.* 2 (Fall):9–11.

1969b "Introduction." *et al.* 2 (Fall):1–2.

Horton, Paul B., and Donald H. Bouma

1970–71 "The sociological reformation: Immolation or rebirth?" *Sociological Focus* 4 (Winter):25–41.

Hoult, Thomas F.

1968 ". . . who shall prepare himself to the battle?" *American Sociologist* 3 (February):3–7.

Huber, Joan

1973 "Symbolic interaction as a pragmatic perspective: The bias of emergent theory." *American Sociological Review* 38 (April):274–84.

Inkeles, Alex

1959 "Personality and social structure." Pp. 249–76 in Robert K. Merton, Leonard Broom, and Leonard Cottrell (eds.), Sociology Today: Problems and Prospects. New York: Basic Books.

1964 What Is Sociology?: An Introduction to the Discipline and Profession. Englewood Cliffs, N.J.: Prentice-Hall.

Insurgent Sociologist
　　1969　Newsletter. Volume 1 (no number or month given).
　　1970　Newsletter. Volume 1, number 3, August.
　　1971　Newsletter. Volume 1, number 4, April.
　1971–72　Bound Periodicals, Volume 2, numbers 1–4 (November–December through Summer).
　1972–73　Bound Periodicals, Volume 3, numbers 1–3 (Summer through Spring).
　1973–74　Bound Periodicals, Volume 4, number 1 (Fall).

Israel, Joachim
　　1972　"Is a non-normative social science possible?" *Acta Sociologica* 15 (1):69–87.

Jacobs, Sue, and Carol Brown
　　1970　"Elaborating the obvious." *Insurgent Sociologist* 1 (August):3, 7.

James, William
　　1890　Principles of Psychology. Two volumes; New York: Holt.

Janowitz, Morris, and Reuben Hill
　　1973　"Internationalizing American sociology through the research committees of the International Sociological Association." *American Sociologist* 8 (May): 77–84.

Jay, Martin
　　1973　The Dialectical Imagination: A History of the Frankfurt School and the Institute of Social Research 1923–1950. New York: Little, Brown.

Johnson, D.
　　1971　"Counter-insurgent study of students protested." *Insurgent Sociologist* 1 (April):3.

Johnson, Harry M.
　　1969　Review of Walter Buckley (ed.), Modern Systems Research for the Behavioral Sciences.

Chicago: Aldine, 1968. In the *American Sociological Review* 34 (February, 1969):102–03.

Kahl, Joseph A. (ed.)
1968 Comparative Perspectives on Stratification: Mexico, Great Britain, Japan. Boston: Little, Brown.

Kahn, Si
1970 How People Get Power: Organizing Oppressed Communities for Action. New York: McGraw-Hill.

Kaplan, Abraham
1964 The Conduct of Inquiry: Methodology for Behavioral Science. San Francisco: Chandler.

Katz, Fred E.
1968 Autonomy and Organization: The Limits of Social Control. New York: Random House.

Keeley, Benjamin J.
1964 "Use of reading lists for graduate students in sociology." *Sociology and Social Research* 18 (July):449–53.

Kelman, Herbert C.
1968 A Time to Speak: On Human Values and Social Research. San Francisco: Jossey-Bass.

Keniston, Kenneth
1968 Young Radicals: Notes on Committed Youth. New York: Harcourt, Brace & World.

Kidron, Michael
1970 Western Capitalism Since the War. Baltimore: Penguin Books.

Kinch, John W.
1963 "A formalized theory of the self concept." *American Journal of Sociology* 68 (January): 481–86.

Klapp, Orrin
>   1973   Models of Social Order: An Introduction to So-
>   ciological Theory. Palo Alto, Calif.: National
>   Press Books.

Koch, Sigmund
>   1964   "Psychology and emerging conceptions of knowl-
>   edge as unitary." Pp. 1–45 in T. W. Wann (ed.),
>   Behaviorism and Phenomenology: Contrasting
>   Bases for Modern Psychology. Chicago and
>   London: University of Chicago Press.

Kuhn, Manford H.
>   1964   "Major trends in symbolic interaction theory in
>   the past twenty-five years." *Sociological Quar-
>   terly* 5 (Winter):61–84.

Kuhn, Thomas S.
>   1962   The Structure of Scientific Revolutions. Chicago
>   and London: University of Chicago Press.
>   1970   The Structure of Scientific Revolutions. Sec-
>   ond ed.; Chicago and London: University of
>   Chicago Press.

Kultgen, John H.
>   1970   "The value of value judgments in sociology."
>   *Sociological Quarterly* 11 (Spring):181–93.

Kunkel, John H.
>   1970   Society and Economic Growth: A Behavioral
>   Perspective of Social Change. New York: Ox-
>   ford University Press.

Kunkel, John H., and Richard H. Nagasawa
>   1973   "A behavioral model of man: Propositions and
>   implications." *American Sociological Review*
>   38 (October):530–43.

Lagos, Gustavo
>   1963   International Stratification and Underdeveloped
>   Countries. Chapel Hill: University of North
>   Carolina Press.

Larson, Calvin J.
1973   Major Themes in Sociological Theory. New York: David McKay.

Lavender, Abraham D., and Robert B. Coates
1972   "Sociological specialties and employment." *American Sociologist* 7 (May):14–15.

Lazarsfeld, Paul F., and Neil W. Henry
1968   Latent Structure Analysis. New York: Houghton-Mifflin.

Lazarsfeld, Paul F., William H. Sewell, and Harold L. Wilensky (eds.)
1967   The Uses of Sociology. New York: Basic Books.

Lee, Alfred M.
1973   Toward Humanist Sociology. Englewood Cliffs, N.J.: Prentice-Hall.

Lefebvre, Henri
1968   The Sociology of Marx. Norbert Guterman, translator; New York: Random House (originally published in 1966).

Lenski, Gerhard E.
1966   Power and Privilege: A Theory of Social Stratification. New York: McGraw-Hill.

Levy, Jr., Marion J.
1952   The Structure of Society. Princeton, N.J.: Princeton University Press.
1963   "Some problems for a unified theory of human nature." Pp. 9–32 in Edward A. Tiryakian (ed.), Sociological Theory, Values, and Sociocultural Change: Essays in Honor of Pitirim A. Sorokin. New York: Free Press of Glencoe.
1966   Modernization and the Structure of Societies: A Setting for International Affairs. Three volumes; Princeton: Princeton University Press.
1968   "Functional analysis: I. Structure-functional analysis." Pp. 21–29 in David Sills (ed.), In-

ternational Encyclopedia of the Social Sciences. Volume 6; New York: Crowell-Collier and Macmillan.

Lichtheim, George
    1965   Marxism: An Historical and Critical Study. Second, revised ed.; New York: Praeger.

Lidz, Victor
    1970   "Values in sociology: A critique of Szymanski's alleged radical view." *Sociological Inquiry* 40 (Winter): 13–20.
    1972   "On the construction of objective theory: Rejoinder to Szymanski." *Sociological Inquiry* 42 (Winter):51–64.

Lipset, Seymour M., and Everett C. Ladd, Jr.
    1972   "The politics of American sociologists," *American Journal of Sociology* 78 (July):67–104.

Lockwood, David
    1958   The Blackcoated Worker: A Study in Class Consciousness. London: Allen and Unwin.
    1964   "Social integration and system integration." Pp. 244–57 in George K. Zollschan and Walter Hirsch (eds.), Explorations in Social Change. Boston: Houghton-Mifflin.

Lofland, John
    1971   Analyzing Social Settings: A Guide to Qualitative Observation and Analysis. Belmont, Calif.: Wadsworth.

Loomis, Charles P.
    1960   Social Systems: Essays on Their Persistence and Change. Princeton, N.J.: Van Nostrand.

Loomis, Charles P., and Zona K. Loomis
    1965   Modern Social Theories: Selected American Writers. Second ed.; Princeton, N.J.: Van Nostrand.

Lukes, Steven
    1970   "Methodological individualism reconsidered." Chapter 5 in Dorothy Emmet and Alasdair Macintyre (eds.), Sociological Theory and Philosophic Analysis. London: Macmillan.

Lundberg, George A.
    1939   Foundations of Sociology. New York: Macmillan.
    1942   Social Research: A Study in Methods of Gathering Data. Second ed.; New York: Longmans, Green.
    1947   Can Science Save Us? New York: Longmans, Green.
    1955   "The natural science trend in sociology." *American Journal of Sociology* 61 (November):191–202.
    1956   "Some convergences in sociological theory." *American Journal of Sociology* 62 (July):21–27.
    1964   Foundations of Sociology. Revised and abridged ed.; New York: David McKay.

Lynd, Robert S.
    1939   Knowledge for What? Princeton: Princeton University Press.

MacIver, Robert M.
    1937   Society: A Textbook of Sociology. New York: Rinehart and Co.
    1942   Social Causation. Boston: Ginn.

MacRae, Jr., Duncan
    1971   "A dilemma of sociology: science versus policy." *American Sociologist* 6 (June):2–7.

Malinowski, Bronislaw
    1922   Argonauts of the Western Pacific: An Account of Native Enterprise in the Archipelagoes of Melanesian New Guinea. London: Routledge and Sons.

1926   Crime and Custom in Savage Society. London: Kegan Paul.
1944   A Scientific Theory of Culture and Other Essays. Chapel Hill; University of North Carolina Press.

Manheim, Ernest
1973   "The drift of alienated students to sociology: an opinion." *American Sociologist* 8 (November):192–95.

Manis, Jerome G., and Bernard N. Meltzer (eds.)
1972   Symbolic Interaction: A Reader in Social Psychology. Second ed.; Boston: Allyn and Bacon.

Mannheim, Karl
1936   Ideology and Utopia: An Introduction to the Sociology of Knowledge. New York: Harcourt, Brace & World (originally published in 1929).

March, James G. (ed.)
1965   Handbook of Organizations. Chicago: Rand McNally.

March, James G., and Herbert A. Simon
1958   Organizations. New York: Wiley.

Marcuse, Herbert
1966   One-Dimensional Man: Studies in the Ideology of Advanced Industrial Society. Boston: Beacon Press (originally published in 1964).

Maris, Ronald
1970   "The logical adequacy of Homans' social theory." *American Sociological Review* 35 (December):1069–81.

Marković, Mihailo
1972   "The problem of reification and the *verstehen-erklären* controversy." *Acta Sociologica* 15 (1): 27–38.

Marsh, Robert M.
1967   Comparative Sociology: A Codification of Cross-Societal Analysis. New York: Harcourt, Brace & World.

Martindale, Don
    1960   The Nature and Types of Sociological Theory. Boston: Houghton-Mifflin.
    1963   Community, Character and Civilization: Studies in Social Behaviorism. New York: Free Press. Chapter 3, "Talcott Parsons' theoretical metamorphosis from social behaviorism to macro functionalism." Chapter originally in *Alpha Kappa Deltan* 29 (Winter):38–46, 1959.

Marx, Karl
    1938   Critique of the Gotha Programme. C. P. Dutt, editor; New York: International Publishers (originally published in 1875).
    1940   The Civil War in France. New York: International Publishers (originally published in 1871).
    1947   The German Ideology, Parts I and III. R. Pascal, editor; New York: International Publishers (originally written in 1845–1846, with Friedrich Engels).
    1964   The Eighteenth Brumaire of Louis Bonaparte. New York: International Publishers (originally published in 1852).
    1967   The Communist Manifesto. Samuel Moore, translator; Baltimore: Penguin (originally published in 1849, with Friedrich Engels).

Marx, Melvin (ed.)
    1963   Theories in Contemporary Psychology. New York: Macmillan.

Mauss, Marcel
    1954   The Gift: Forms and Functions of Exchange in Archaic Societies. Ian Cunnison, translator; London: Cohen and West.

Mayrl, William W.
    1973   "Phenomenology and interactionism: A case against synthesis." Paper given in theory section, Midwest Sociological Society meetings, April 27.

McEwen, William P.
  1963   The Problem of Social-Scientific Knowledge. Totowa, N.J.: Bedminster Press.

McGinnis, Robert
  1965   Mathematical Foundations for Social Analysis. Indianapolis: Bobbs-Merrill.

McHugh, Peter
  1968   Defining the Situation: The Organization of Meaning in Social Interaction. Indianapolis: Bobbs-Merrill.
  1970   "On the failure of positivism." Chapter 14 in Douglas (ed.), 1970, op. cit.

McKee, James B.
  1970–71 "The radical challenge to sociology." *Sociological Focus* 4 (Winter):6–14.

McKinney, John C.
  1966   Constructive Typology and Social Theory. New York: Appleton-Century-Crofts.
  1970   "Sociological theory and the process of typification." Chapter 9 in John C. McKinney and Edward A. Tiryakian (eds.), Theoretical Sociology: Perspectives and Developments. New York: Appleton-Century-Crofts.

McKinney, John C., and Edward A. Tiryakian (eds.)
  1970   Theoretical Sociology: Perspectives and Developments. New York: Appleton-Century-Crofts.

Mead, George H.
  1934   Mind, Self and Society: From the Standpoint of a Social Behaviorist. Charles W. Morris, editor; Chicago: University of Chicago Press.
  1964   On Social Psychology: Selected Papers. Anselm L. Strauss, editor; Chicago: University of Chicago Press, Phoenix edition.

Meadows, Paul
  1967   "The metaphors of order: Toward a taxonomy of organization." Pp. 77–103 in Gross (ed.), 1967, op. cit.

Meeker, B. F.
1971   "Decisions and exchange." *American Sociological Review* 36 (June):485–95.

Meltzer, Bernard N.
1959   The Social Psychology of George Herbert Mead. Kalamazoo, Mich.: Center for Sociological Research at Western Michigan University.

Meltzer, Bernard N., and John W. Petras
1970   "The Chicago and Iowa schools of symbolic interactionism." Pp. 3–17 in Tamotsu Shibutani (ed.), Human Nature and Collective Behavior: Papers in Honor of Herbert Blumer. Englewood Cliffs, N.J.: Prentice Hall.

Merton, Robert K.
1949   Social Theory and Social Structure. Glencoe, Ill.: Free Press.
1957a "The role-set: Problems in sociological theory." *British Journal of Sociology* 8 (June):106–20.
1957b Social Theory and Social Structure. Revised and enlarged ed.; Glencoe, Ill.: Free Press.
1967   On Theoretical Sociology: Five Essays, Old and New. New York: Free Press.
1968   Social Theory and Social Structure. Enlarged, third ed.; Glencoe, Ill.: Free Press.

Merton, Robert K., Leonard Broom, and Leonard S. Cottrell, Jr. (eds.)
1959   Sociology Today: Problems and Prospects. New York: Basic Books.

Mihanovitch, Clement S., and others (eds.)
1957   Glossary of Sociological Terms. Milwaukee: Bruce.

Miliband, Ralph
1969   The State in Capitalist Society. London: Weidenfeld & Nicholson.

Mills, C. Wright
1943   "The professional ideology of social pathol-

ogists." *American Journal of Sociology* 49 (September):165–80.

1956   The Power Elite. New York: Oxford University Press.

1959   The Sociological Imagination. New York: Oxford University Press.

1962   The Marxists. New York: Dell.

Mills, Theodore M.

1959   "Equilibrium and the processes of deviance and control." *American Sociological Review* 24 (October):671–79.

Mitchell, G. Duncan

1968   A Dictionary of Sociology. London: Routledge & Kegan Paul.

Miyamoto, Frank S.

1971   "Self, motivation, and symbolic interactionist theory." Pp. 271–85 in Tamotsu Shibutani (ed.), Human Nature and Collective Behavior: Papers in Honor of Herbert Blumer. Englewood Cliffs, N.J.: Prentice-Hall.

Moore, Jr., Barrington

1958   Political Power and Social Theory. Cambridge, Mass.: Harvard University Press.

Moore, Wilbert E.

1960   "A reconsideration of theories of social change." *American Sociological Review* 25 (December): 810–18.

1963   Social Change. Englewood Cliffs, N.J.: Prentice-Hall.

1967   (ed.) Order and Change: Essays in Comparative Sociology. New York: Wiley.

Mouzelis, Nicos P.

1967   Organizations and Bureaucracy: An Analysis of Modern Theories. London: Routledge.

Mullins, Nicholas C.

1971   The Art of Theory: Construction and Use. New York: Harper & Row.

1973   Theories and Theory Groups in Contemporary American Sociology. New York: Harper & Row.

Myrdal, Gunnar
1944   An American Dilemma: The Negro Problem and Modern Democracy. New York: Harper. (assisted by Richard Sterner and Arnold Rose)
1969   Objectivity in Social Research. New York: Pantheon.

Nagel, Ernest
1961   The Structure of Science: Problems in the Logic of Scientific Explanation. New York: Harcourt, Brace & World.

Natanson, Maurice
1956   The Social Dynamics of George H. Mead. Washington, D.C.: Public Affairs Press.
1963   (ed.) Philosophy of the Social Sciences. New York: Random House.
1972   "Phenomenology and social role." *Journal of the British Society for Phenomenology* 3 (October): 218–30.

Nettl, J. P., and Roland Robertson
1968   International Systems and the Modernization of Societies. New York: Basic Books.

Nettler, Gwynn
1972   "Knowing and doing." *American Sociologist* 7 (February): 3, 5–7.

Nicolaus, Martin
1969   "Remarks at ASA convention." *American Sociologist* 4 (May):154–56.

Nisbet, Robert A.
1966   The Sociological Tradition. New York: Basic Books.
1968   Tradition and Revolt: Historical and Sociological Essays. New York: Random House.

Oberschall, Anthony
1972   "The institutionalization of American sociology." Pp. 187–251 in Anthony Oberschall (ed.), The

Establishment of Empirical Sociology: Studies in Continuity, Discontinuity, and Institutionalization. New York: Harper & Row.

O'Donnell, L.
1971   "West Coast Indians battle for rights." *Insurgent Sociologist* 1 (April):1, 4.

Odum, Howard W.
1947   Understanding Society: The Principles of Dynamic Sociology. New York: Macmillan.

Ogburn, William F.
1922   Social Change, with Respect to Culture and Original Nature. New York: Viking Press.

Olsen, Marvin E.
1968   The Process of Social Organization. New York: Holt, Rinehart & Winston.

O'Neill, John
1970   "Sociology as a skin trade." *Sociological Inquiry* 40 (Winter):101–104.
1972   "The new sociology and the advent of Alvin W. Gouldner." Review article; *Canadian Review of Sociology and Anthropology* 9 (2):167–75.

Oppenheimer, Martin
1970   "Another view of a New Left panel discussant." Letter; *American Sociologist* 5:45.
1971   "Nationalist praxis." *Insurgent Sociologist* 1 (April):7–8.

Orlans, Harold
1973   Contracting for Knowledge. San Francisco: Jossey-Bass.

Oromaner, Mark
1968   "The most cited sociologists: An analysis of introductory text citations." *American Sociologist* 3 (May):124–26.
1969   "The audience as a determinant of the most important sociologists." *American Sociologist* 4 (November):332–35.

1972 "The structure of influence in contemporary academic sociology." *American Sociologist* 7 (May):11–13.

Ossowski, Stanislaw

1963 Class Structure in the Social Consciousness. Sheila Patterson, translator; New York: Free Press (originally published in 1957). Referred to in Lenski, 1966, op. cit.

Park, Peter

1969 Sociology, Tomorrow: An Evaluation of Sociological Theories in Terms of Science. New York: Pegasus.

Parsons, Talcott

1937 The Structure of Social Action: A Study in Social Theory with Special Reference to a Group of Recent European Writers. New York: McGraw-Hill.

1945 "The present position and prospects of systematic theory in sociology." Chapter 3 in Georges Gurvitch and Wilbert E. Moore (eds.), Twentieth Century Sociology. New York: Philosophical Library. Also reprinted in the author's Essays in Sociological Theory. Revised; Glencoe, Ill.: Free Press, 1954, Chapter 11.

1951 The Social System. Glencoe, Ill.: Free Press.

1959a "An approach to psychological theory in terms of the theory of action." Pp. 647–51 in Sigmund Koch (ed.), Psychology: A Study of a Science. Volume 3; New York: McGraw-Hill.

1959b "General theory in sociology." Pp. 3–38 in Merton, Broom, and Cottrell (eds.), 1959, op. cit.

1960 Structure and Process in Modern Societies. Glencoe, Ill.: Free Press (first two chapters published originally in 1956 and 1958, respectively).

1961a "An outline of the social system." Pp. 30–79 in Talcott Parsons, Edward A. Shils, Kaspar D.

Naegele, and Jesse R. Pitts (eds.), Theories of Society: Foundations of Modern Sociological Theory. Volume 1; New York: Free Press.

1961b   "The point of view of the author." Pp. 311–63 in Max Black (ed.), 1961, op. cit.

1966   Societies: Evolutionary and Comparative Perspectives. Englewood Cliffs, N.J.: Prentice-Hall.

1967   Sociological Theory and Modern Society. New York: Free Press.

1969   Politics and Social Structure. New York: Free Press.

1970   "Some problems of general theory in sociology." Pp. 27–68 in McKinney and Tiryakian (eds.), 1970, op. cit.

1971   The System of Modern Societies. Englewood Cliffs, N.J.: Prentice-Hall.

1972   "Culture and social system revisited." *Social Science Quarterly* 53 (September):253–66.

Parsons, Talcott, Robert F. Bales, and Edward A. Shils

1953   Working Papers in the Theory of Action. Glencoe, Ill.: Free Press.

Parsons, Talcott, Robert F. Bales, and others

1955   Family, Socialization and Interaction Process. Glencoe, Ill.: Free Press.

Parsons, Talcott, and Edward A. Shils (eds.)

1951   Toward a General Theory of Action: Theoretical Foundations for the Social Sciences. New York: Harper.

Parsons, Talcott, Edward A. Shils, Kaspar D. Naegele, and Jesse R. Pitts (eds.)

1961   Theories of Society: Foundations of Modern Sociological Theory. Two volumes; New York: Free Press.

Pepper, Stephen C.

1966   World Hypotheses: A Study in Evidence. Berkeley and Los Angeles: University of California Press (originally published in 1942).

Phillips, Derek L.
1973 Abandoning Method: Sociological Studies in Methodology. San Francisco: Jossey-Bass.

Pivčević, Edo
1972 "Can there be a phenomenological sociology?" *Sociology* (Great Britain) 6 (September):335–49.

Podell, Lawrence, Martin Vogelfanger, and Roberta Rogers
1959 "Sociology in American colleges: Fifteen years later." *American Sociological Review* 24 (February):87–95.

Ponsioen, Johannes A.
1968 National Development: A Sociological Contribution. New York: Humanities Press.

Porter, Jack N.
1971 "Talking police blues: Pedagogic dilemma of the academic." *Insurgent Sociologist* 1 (April): 6–7.
1973 "Purge of radical sociologists." *Footnotes* 1 (May):3.

Price, James L.
1968 Organizational Effectiveness: An Inventory of Propositions. Homewood, Ill.: Irwin.

Przeworski, Adam, and Henry Teune
1970 The Logic of Comparative Social Inquiry. New York: Wiley-Interscience.

Psathas, George (ed.)
1973 Phenomenological Sociology: Issues and Applications. New York: Wiley-Interscience.

Reid, Sue T., and Alan P. Bates
1971 "Undergraduate sociology programs in accredited colleges and universities." *American Sociologist* 6 (May):165–75.

Remmling, Gunter W.
    1967   Road to Suspicion: A Study of Modern Mentality and the Sociology of Knowledge. New York: Appleton-Century-Crofts.

Rex, John
    1961   Key Problems of Sociological Theory. London: Routledge & Kegan Paul.

Reynolds, Larry T., and Bernard N. Meltzer
    1973   "The origins of divergent methodological stances in symbolic interactionism." *Sociological Quarterly* 14 (Spring):189–99.

Reynolds, Larry T., and Janice M. Reynolds (eds.)
    1970   The Sociology of Sociology: Analysis and Criticism of the Thought, Research, and Ethical Folkways of Sociology and Its Practitioners. New York: David McKay.

Reynolds, Paul D.
    1971   A Primer in Theory Construction. Indianapolis: Bobbs-Merrill.

Riley, Matilda W.
    1960   "Membership of the American Sociological Association, 1950–1959." *American Sociological Review* 25 (December):914–26.

Roach, Jack L.
    1967   "A theory of lower-class behavior." Pp. 294–314 in Gross (ed.), 1967, op. cit.
    1970   "The radical sociology movement: A short history and commentary." *American Sociologist* 5 (August):224–33.

Robbins, Richard
    1969   "Who will liberate the Sociology Liberation Movement?" *American Sociologist* 4 (May):156–58.

Rose, Arnold M.
    1954   Theory and Method in the Social Sciences. Minneapolis: University of Minnesota Press.

1962   (ed.) Human Behavior and Social Processes:
        An Interactionist Approach. Boston: Houghton-
        Mifflin.
1967   "The relation of theory and method." Pp. 207–
        19 in Gross (ed.), 1967, op. cit.
1969   "Varieties of sociological imagination." *Ameri-
        can Sociological Review* (Oct.):623–30. (1969
        posthumous presidential address, American
        Sociological Association)

Rosenberg, Bernard
1972   The Province of Sociology: Freedom and Con-
        straint. New York: Crowell.

Rossi, Peter H.
1970–71 "Beyond cultural relativity: The place of values
        in social science." *Sociological Focus* 4 (Win-
        ter):121–31.

Rothman, Robert A.
1971   "Textbooks and the certification of knowledge."
        American Sociologist 6 (May):125–27.

Roucek, Joseph S. (ed.)
1958   Contemporary Sociology. New York: Philo-
        sophical Library.

Rubenstein, Albert N., and Chadwick J. Haberstroh (eds.)
1966   Some Theories of Organization. Second ed.;
        Homewood, Ill.: Irwin.

Sallach, David L.
1973a   "Critical theory and critical sociology: the sec-
        ond synthesis. *Sociological Inquiry* 43 (Spring):
        131–40.
1973b   "What is sociological theory?" *American Soci-
        ologist* 8 (August):134–39.

Schafer, Robert B.
1973   "Exchange and symbolic interaction: A further
        analysis of convergence." Paper given in theory
        section, Midwest Sociological Society meetings,
        April 27.

222   *References*

Scheffler, Israel
 1963 The Anatomy of Inquiry. New York: Knopf.
Schermerhorn, Richard A., and Alvin W. Boskoff
 1957 "Recent analyses of sociological theory." Chapter 3 in Becker and Boskoff (eds.), 1957, op. cit.
Schevitz, Jeffrey M.
 1970 "Irving show goes sour in St. Louis." *Insurgent Sociologist* 1 (August):5.
 1971 "The reviewer replies." In "Commentary and Debate"; *American Journal of Sociology* 77 (September):305–6.
Schnore, Leo F.
 1958 "Social morphology and human ecology." *American Journal of Sociology* 63 (May):620–34.
Schrag, Clarence
 1967 "Elements of theoretical analysis in sociology." Pp. 220–53 in Gross (ed.), 1967, op. cit.
Scott, John F.
 1963 "The changing foundations of the Parsonian action scheme." *American Sociological Review* 28 (October):716–35.
Scott, W. Richard
 1964 "Theory of organizations." Chapter 14 in Faris (ed.), 1964, op. cit.
Scriven, Michael
 1961 "The key property of physical laws—inaccuracy." Pp. 91–101 in Herbert Feigl and Grover Maxwell (eds.), Current Issues in the Philosophy of Science. New York: Holt, Rinehart & Winston.
 1964 "Views of human nature." Pp. 163–90 in T. W. Wann (ed.), Behaviorism and Phenomenology: Contrasting Bases for Modern Psychology. Chicago and London: University of Chicago Press.

Sewell, William H.
1971 "Students and the university." *American So-ciologist* 6 (May):111–17.

Shaw, Marvin E., and Philip R. Costanzo
1970 Theories of Social Psychology. New York: McGraw-Hill.

Sibley, Elbridge
1971 "Scientific sociology at bay?" *American Sociolo-gist* 6 (June, Supplementary Issue):13–17.

Simmel, Georg
1950 The Sociology of Georg Simmel. Kurt H. Wolff, editor; Glencoe, Ill.: Free Press.
1955 Conflict and the Web of Group-Affiliations. Kurt H. Wolff and Reinhard Bendix, translators; London: Collier-Macmillan Ltd., Free Press of Glencoe.

Simpson, Richard L.
1961 "Expanding and declining fields in American sociology." *American Sociological Review* 26 (June):458–66.

Singlemann, Peter
1972 "Exchange as symbolic interaction: Convergence between two theoretical perspectives." *American Sociological Review* 37 (August):414–24.

Sjoberg, Gideon (ed.)
1967 Ethics, Politics, and Social Research. Cambridge, Mass.: Schenkman.

Sjoberg, Gideon, and Roger Nett
1968 A Methodology for Social Research. New York: Harper & Row.

Small, Albion W.
1905 General Sociology: An Exposition of the Main Developments in Sociological Theory from Spencer to Ratzenhofer. Chicago: University of Chicago Press.

Smelser, Neil
    1963   Theory of Collective Behavior. New York: Free Press.
    1968   Essays in Sociological Explanation. Englewood Cliffs, N.J.: Prentice-Hall.

Smith, Dusky L.
    1964   "The sunshine boys: Toward a sociology of happiness." *The Activist* (Spring):166–67.

Sonquist, John A.
    1970   Multivariate Model Building: The Validation of a Search Strategy. Ann Arbor: Institute for Social Research, University of Michigan.

Sorokin, Pitirim A.
    1928   Contemporary Sociological Theories. New York: Harper.
1937–41   Social and Cultural Dynamics. Four volumes; New York: American Book Company.
    1941   The Crisis of Our Age. New York: Dutton.
    1950   Social Philosophies of an Age of Crisis. Boston: Beacon Press.
    1956   Fads and Foibles in Modern Sociology and Related Sciences. Chicago: H. Regnery Company.
    1958   "Physicalist and mechanistic school." Pp. 1127–71 in Roucek (ed.), 1958, op. cit.
    1965   "Sociology of yesterday, today and tomorrow." *American Sociological Review* 30 (December):833–43.
    1966   Sociological Theories of Today. New York: Harper & Row.

Spencer, Martin E.
    1971   "Conflict and the neutrals." *Sociological Quarterly* 12 (Spring):219–31.

Sperber, Irwin
    1970   "Is radical sociology an organization?" *Insurgent Sociologist* 1 (August):3, 7.

Spinrad, William
 1972 "The politics of T. R. Young." Letter; *American Sociologist* 7 (May):4, 17.

Stark, Werner
 1963 The Fundamental Forms of Social Thought. New York: Fordham University Press.

Stehr, Nico, and Lyle E. Larson
 1972 "The rise and decline of areas of specialization." *American Sociologist* 7 (August):3, 5–6.

Stein, Maurice R., and Arthur J. Vidich (eds.)
 1963 Sociology on Trial. Englewood Cliffs, N.J.: Prentice-Hall.

Stinchcombe, Arthur L.
 1968 Constructing Social Theories. New York: Harcourt, Brace & World.

Stone, Gregory P., and Harvey A. Farberman (eds.)
 1970 Social Psychology through Symbolic Interaction. Waltham, Mass.: Ginn-Blaisdell.

Stoodley, Bartlett H. (ed.)
 1962 Society and Self: A Reader in Social Psychology. New York: Free Press.

Strauss, Anselm L., Leonard Schatzman, Danuta Ehrlich, Rue Bucher, and Melvin Sabshin
 1963 "The hospital and its negotiated order." Pp. 147–69 in Eliot Freidson (ed.), The Hospital in Modern Society. New York: Free Press of Glencoe.

Stryker, Sheldon
 1964 "The interactional and situational approach." Chapter 4 in Harold T. Christensen (ed.), Handbook of Marriage and the Family. Chicago: Rand McNally.

Sudnow, David (ed.)
 1972 Studies in Social Interaction. New York: Free Press.

Sumner, William G.
> 1911   War and Other Essays. New Haven: Yale University Press.

Szymanski, Albert
> 1970a   "On ideological struggle." *Insurgent Sociologist* 1 (August):3, 7–8.
> 1970b   "Toward a radical sociology." *Sociological Inquiry* 40 (Winter):3–13.
> 1970c   "The value of sociology: An answer to Lidz." *Sociological Inquiry* 40 (Winter):21–25.
> 1972   "Dialectical functionalism: A further answer to Lidz." *Sociological Inquiry* 42 (Spring):145–53.
> 1973   "Marxism and science." *Insurgent Sociologist* 3 (Spring):25–38.

Tarde, Gabriel
> 1899   Social Laws. Harry C. Warren, translator; New York: Macmillan.

Tarter, Donald E.
> 1973   "Heeding Skinner's call: toward the development of a social technology," *American Sociologist* 8 (November):153–58.

Theodorson, George A., and Achilles G. Theodorson
> 1969   A Modern Dictionary of Sociology. New York: Crowell.

Thibaut, John W., and Harold H. Kelley
> 1959   The Social Psychology of Groups. New York: Wiley.

Timasheff, Nicholas S.
> 1952   "The basic concepts of sociology." *American Journal of Sociology* 58 (September):176–86.
> 1957   Sociological Theory: Its Nature and Growth. Revised ed.; New York: Random House.
> 1967   Sociological Theory: Its Nature and Growth. Third ed.; New York: Random House.

Tiryakian, Edward A.
> 1962   Sociologism and Existentialism: Two Perspec-

tives on the Individual and Society. Englewood Cliffs, N.J.: Prentice-Hall.

1965   "Existential phenomenology and the sociological tradition." *American Sociological Review* 30 (October):674–88.

Toby, Jackson
1971   "A criticism of Colfax's review of Parsons." *American Journal of Sociology* 77 (September): 306–8.

Turk, Herman, and Richard L. Simpson (eds.)
1971   Institutions and Social Exchange. Indianapolis: Bobbs-Merrill.

Turner, Damon A.
1970   "Survival or suicide." Letter; *American Sociologist* 5 (February):43–44.

Turner, Jonathan H.
1974   The Structure of Sociological Theory. Homewood, Ill.: Dorsey Press.

Tyrmand, Leopold
1970   Notebooks of a Dilettante. New York: Macmillan.

Van den Berghe, Pierre L.
1963   "Dialectic and functionalism: Toward a theoretical synthesis." *American Sociological Review* 28 (October):695–705.

1971   "The benign quota: Panacea or Pandora's box." *American Sociologist* 6 (June, Supplementary Issue):40–43.

Van den Haag, Ernest
1963   Passion and Social Constraint. New York: Stein & Day.

Vaughan, Ted R.
1967   "Governmental intervention in social research: Political and ethical dimensions in the Wichita jury recordings." Chapter 3 in Sjoberg (ed.), 1967, op. cit.

Vidich, Arthur J., and Joseph Bensman
1964   "The Springdale case: Academic bureaucrats and sensitive townspeople." Pp. 313–49 in Arthur J. Vidich, Joseph Bensman, and Maurice R. Stein (eds.), Reflections on Community Studies. New York: Wiley.

Vold, George B.
1958   Theoretical Criminology. New York: Oxford University Press.

Wagner, Helmut R.
1963   "Types of sociological theory: Toward a system of classification." *American Sociological Review* 28 (October):735–42.
1964   "Displacement of scope: a problem of the relationship between small-scale and large-scale sociological theories." *American Journal of Sociology* 69 (May):571–84.
1974   "Signs, symbols, and interaction theory." *Sociological Focus* 7 (Spring):101–11.

Wallace, Anthony F. C.
1970   Culture and Personality. Second ed.; New York: Random House.

Wallace, Walter L.
1969   (ed.) Sociological Theory: An Introduction. Chicago: Aldine.
1971   The Logic of Science in Sociology. Chicago: Aldine-Atherton.

Wann, T. W. (ed.)
1964   Behaviorism and Phenomenology: Contrasting Bases for Modern Psychology. Chicago and London: University of Chicago Press.

Ward, Thomas J.
1974   "Definitions of theory in sociology." Chapter 1 in R. Serge Denisoff, Orel Callahan, and Mark H. Levine (eds.), 1974, op. cit.

Warshay, Leon H.
> 1971a "The current state of sociological theory." *Sociological Quarterly* 12 (Winter):23–45.
>
> 1971b "A typology for modern sociological theories: Diversity and polarity in search of order." *Sociology and Social Research* 55 (January):203–15.

Webb, Eugene J., Donald T. Campbell, Richard S. Schwartz, and Lee Sechrest
> 1966 Unobtrusive Measures: Nonreactive Research in the Social Sciences. Chicago: Rand McNally.

Weber, Max
> 1949 Max Weber on the Methodology of the Social Sciences. Edward A. Shils and Henry A. Finch, translators and editors; Glencoe, Ill.: Free Press.

Westie, Frank R.
> 1957 "Toward closer relations between theory and research: A procedure and an example." *American Sociological Review* 22 (April):149–54.

Willems, David
> 1973 "A reply to Ted Goertzel's article, 'Class and politics in the 1970's.'" *Insurgent Sociologist* 4 (Fall):65–72.

Willer, David, and Judith Willer
> 1973 Systematic Empiricism: Critique of a Pseudoscience. Englewood Cliffs, N.J.: Prentice-Hall.

Willhelm, Sidney M.
> 1973 "The political economy of professional sociology: The emergence of underdevelopment in the undergraduate sociology program." *Insurgent Sociologist* 4 (Fall):15–28.

Williams, Jr., Robin M.
> 1951 American Society: A Sociological Interpretation. New York: Knopf.

1961   "The sociological theory of Talcott Parsons."
        Pp. 64–99 in Black (ed.), 1961, op. cit.
1970   American Society: A Sociological Interpretation.
        Third ed.; New York: Knopf.

Wilson, Thomas P.
1970a   "Conceptions of interaction and forms of so-
        ciological explanation." *American Sociological
        Review* 35 (August):697–710.
1970b   "Normative and interpretive paradigms in so-
        ciology." Chapter 3 in Douglas (ed.), 1970, op.
        cit.

Winch, Robert F.
1963   The Modern Family. Revised ed.; New York:
        Holt, Rinehart & Winston.

Winthrop, Henry
1971   "Some relations between a value-free sociology
        and value-oriented sociologists." Letter; *Ameri-
        can Sociologist* 6 (August):261–62.

Wittgenstein, Ludwig
1953   Philosophical Investigations. G. E. M. Ans-
        combe, translator; New York: Macmillan.

Wrong, Dennis
1961   "The oversocialized conception of man in mod-
        ern sociology." *American Sociological Review*
        26 (April):183–93.
1963   "Human nature and the perspective of sociology."
        Social Research 30 (Autumn):300–318.
1971   "New wine in old bottles—a review of two
        books." *American Sociologist* 6 (August):249–
        52.
1974   "On thinking about the future." *American So-
        ciologist* 9 (February):26–31.

Young, T. R.
1972   New Sources of Self. New York: Pergamon
        Press.

Zeitlin, Irving M.
1968   Ideology and the Development of Sociological Theory. Englewood Cliffs, N.J.: Prentice-Hall.
1972   Capitalism and Imperialism: An Introduction to Neo-Marxian Concepts. Chicago: Markham.

Zeitlin, Maurice
1967   Revolutionary Politics and the Cuban Working Class. Princeton: Princeton University Press.

Zetterberg, Hans L.
1954   On Theory and Verification in Sociology. Stockholm: Almquist & Wiksell.
1965   On Theory and Verification in Sociology. Third ed.; Totowa, N.J.: Bedminster Press.

Znaniecki, Florian
1934   The Method of Sociology. New York: Rinehart.

Zurcher, Jr., Louis A.
1970–71   "Some reflections on sociology and the counterculture." *Sociological Focus* 4 (Winter):61–68.

Zwerman, William L.
1970   New Perspectives on Organization Theory: An Empirical Reconsideration of the Marxian and Classical Analyses. Westport, Conn.: Greenwood.

Name Index

Name Index

Subject Index

Subject Index